D1222423

HERBERT READ

HERBERT READ
by Gregorio Prieto

HERBERT READ

an introduction to his work
by various hands

edited by

HENRY TREECE

KENNIKAT PRESS, INC./PORT WASHINGTON, N. Y.

828.91
R283xt

First published 1944
Reissued 1969 by Kennikat Press

Library of Congress Catalog Card No: 68-26217
Manufactured in the United States of America

CONTENTS

HENRY TREECE

INTRODUCTION

'This thing we call existence; is it not a something which has its roots far down below in the dark, and its branches stretching out into the immensity above, which we among the branches cannot see? Not a chance jumble; a living thing, a *One*. . . .

'And so, it comes to pass in time, that the earth ceases for us to be a weltering chaos. We walk in the great hall of life, looking up and down reverentially. Nothing is despicable—all is meaning-full; nothing is small—all is part of a whole, whose beginning and end we know not. The life that throbs in us is a pulsation from it; too mighty for our comprehension, not too small.

'And so, it comes to pass at last, that whereas the sky was at first a small blue rag stretched out over us, and so low that our hands might touch it, pressing down on us, it raises itself into an immeasurable blue arch over our heads, and we begin to live again.'

The Story of an African Farm, OLIVE SCHREINER

'I salute him as a poet, a critic, a scholar, a philosopher, a prose-writer of distinction.'
GEOFFREY FABER

'The laws of Nature are physical laws: they can be grouped under such general terms as rhythm, proportion, balance, precision, economy, etc.'
HERBERT READ

'Artistic inevitability lies in the complete adequacy of the external to the emotion.'
T. S. ELIOT

I

On September 3rd, 1939, Mr Chamberlain spoke words which indicated the end of many attitudes, many habits of mind and body born and developed during the preceding twenty years of peace; words which, by implication, at the same time announced the birth of new habits of mind and body, new attitudes, to be recognised and nurtured during the years of war and afterwards.

By war comes rebirth; a reassessment and a renunciation, but also, in a civilised world, an incorporation in the new structure of those elements from the old which have shown themselves to be of permanent and fundamental value.

It is a human habit to set the house in order by changing the nature of that order; to cultivate the garden by altering its layout, even its character; and, unfortunately, to turn the head as the water rushes down the pipe, only to find later that the baby is no longer in the bath.

Political and economic reassessment are only two phases of a wide critical attitude; literary reassessment of what the last two decades have produced is yet another phase, and to the writer, one of the first importance. To that reader also for whom literature is a reflection of life, an erection of laws from experience, is such a reassessment invaluable.

And, looking back on the days since Versailles, it is easy now to see through the masks, the gestures and the disguises; it is a simple matter to locate among the crowd that lines the literary corridor, those with feet of clay which, only a matter of five years ago, were so well-camouflaged by the smartest of fashionable shoes.

There is, as I have observed, always the danger of rejecting the good with the bad, or at least, with the less good, and this especially in poetry, perhaps the most confusingly *fashionable* of the arts. There can be, however, little danger of our rejecting those elements of good which can proclaim their quality now with a voice as strong and as pure as at any time during these last twenty chaotic years.

We must not lose this strength, this purity of vision; we shall need these attributes in our teachers in the difficult years that are yet to come. And it is one of the duties of our critics now to find for us the teachers who shall possess these attributes.

There are but few of them, and these often without honour. So that we may know in time where the paths of experience and imagination may lead us in the days of despair and reconstruction, let us honour these minds that have won through a period of time unparalleled in its turbulence, in its conflicting ideologies, by any other period in the world's history.

Let us, among others who will be less worthy, reconsider the work of Herbert Read, as poet, critic and philosopher. It seems to me as inevitable as is Read's work itself that, sooner or later, a book should be written about him. Yet, paradoxically enough, it is perhaps that very quality of inevitability that has so far been mainly responsible for this poet's lack of consideration. Just as the movements of a naturally graceful person are observed, but taken for granted, so Read's poetry, which exists because of its own rights as *poetry* and not as posture or propaganda, has tended to be overlooked because of its very virtue.

8

It is significant that Read should say this of Blake:

'For me, Blake is absolute. Shakespeare is richer, Milton is more sonorous, Hopkins is more sensuous. . . . but Blake has no need of qualifying epithets; he is simply poetic, in imagination and expression.'

These words, if I understand them, constitute the highest praise a writer may be offered, for they signify no less than that he has achieved himself in the fullest degree, as artist and man; that he has come near to solving those emotional and intellectual problems, those psycho-physical dilemmas, which are responsible in their irresolute state for such tensions as produce, on the one hand, the extravagances of Hopkins, and, on the other, the skeletal incoherence of, say, the early Hugh Sykes Davies.

These examples will perhaps show more clearly what I mean:

> 'Tom—garlanded with squat and surly steel
> Tom; then Tom's fallowbootfellow piles pick
> By him and rips out rockfire homeforth—sturdy Dick';
>
> *Tom's Garland*, G. M. HOPKINS

> BABAL   BASALT
> rears mortar'd blocks
> out—boulders
> 100 slave hacked'
>
> *Myth*, H. S. DAVIES

Now, that I have selected a passage from Hugh Sykes Davies' undergraduate work is no misrepresentation, since it is used as a clinical exhibit of adolescent self-repression, which by contrast with a piece of Read's recent work, serves to show all the more clearly the mature sanity and balance both of the latter's insight and of his technical approach:

> ' Descend into the valley
> explore the plain
> even the salt sea
> but keep the heart
> cool in the memory
> of ivy, ash
> and the glistening beck
> running swiftly through the black rocks.'
>
> *The Ivy and the Ash*, H. READ

There is no need to go, for extra emphasis, to the more eccentric British or American poets, for this poem shows as clearly as any that self-conquest, that balanced erection of laws from the multitudinous rubble of the surrounding worlds of Inner and Outer, which also characterise the Blake of *Songs of Experience*, and on the evidence of which Read himself accords to Blake the compliment of 'simply poetic'. In this consideration of Read's maturity, the inevitability of his thought and expression, there is a statement by T. S. Eliot which seems to me apposite. It says,

'The only way of expressing emotion in the form of art is by finding an *objective correlative*; in other words, a set of objects, a situation, a chain of events which shall be the formula of that particular emotion: such that when the external facts, which must terminate in sensory experience, are given, the emotion is immediately evoked. If you examine any of Shakespeare's more successful tragedies, you will find this *exact equivalence*. . .'

Those of us who, during the decade 1930–1940, have observed the reactions to this fundamental law of such poets as Auden and George Barker will have seen in the one a frequently unimaginative adherence which has resulted in a school of mechanistic writing previously inconceivable in English, though possible in French; and in the other, a form of contra-reaction, what Spender has called 'a magnificent ignorance', an inconsequential chaos often uninformed by vision, unrivalled outside the ranks of surrealism.

Read's position, relative to Eliot's concept, can best be shown in his own self-elucidatory words, from *Annals of Innocence and Experience*:

'. . . I think I may say that by the end of the war I had discovered myself and my style—that is to say, I had made an equation between emotion and image, between feeling and expression. So long as I was true to this equation, I need not be afraid of influences or acquired mannerisms. Poetry was reduced to an instrument of precision. "Reduced" will imply, of course, a lack of bulk: from that time my output of verse was to be severely restricted. But what I wrote I tended to keep: I no longer destroyed a large part of my writing. Criticism had become innate, composition an instinctive language; and though I am very far from claiming perfection or permanence for the poems I have retained, I do not think it will be necessary for a reader of the future to approach my work with squared shoulders: he can accept or reject me on the instant. By this statement I lay myself open to the charge that there is nothing in my poetry to detain the reader; but that, of course, is not what I mean. One of the essential characteristics of poetry is what Coleridge called "the power of reducing multitude into unity of effect". Whatever the nature of poetry, be it lyrical or dramatic, meditative or philosophical, this unity of effect should exist, and be immediately apparent. If that unity is achieved, the poem has that quality which is possessed by all true works of art—the quality of retaining our interest in spite of familiarity.'

The choice of quotation from Coleridge is once more significant, as evocative as Blake's grain of sand. It is the undemonstrative admission of a man who has seen his world clearly and cleanly, who has acted organically according to what he has seen, who has absorbed both sight and act into his conception of the universe, and, for the purposes of his art, has condensed and elevated this conception in an imagery which has that *unfailing* air of all permanent things; and all this, in spite of the poet's modest words about his permanence. For Read's permanence is already a poetic entity, the undeniable aura that surrounds all honest statements of belief coming from a mind which has trained itself to be a completely efficient recording instrument.

Once again, there are words by Eliot, from his essay on Blake, with which I would identify Read, as being a sharer of the 'peculiar honesty' which the critic is discussing.

'Nothing that can be called morbid or abnormal or perverse, none of the things which exemplify the sickness of an epoch or a fashion, have this quality; only those things, which, by some *extraordinary labour of simplification*, exhibit the essential sickness or strength of the human soul. And this honesty never exists without great technical accomplishment.'

Those who know anything at all of Read's critical or political philosophy will need no reminder of his honesty of purpose; his true simplicity, his fidelity of statement.

His poetic honesty is the artistic exemplification of Eliot's words in the fullest sense, an honesty which is as technical as ideological. And here I would like to quote from one of Read's short poems, *Summer Rain*, where, I am convinced, a small facet of this honesty can be seen in the poet's abandonment of the poetic form which he had chosen.

This poem consists of seven three-lined verses, six of which are quite formal in their rhyme or half-rhyme; the remaining stanza, however, the fifth, suddenly disobeys the preordained scheme, in such a way as to produce something like a small shock:

'Against the window pane
against the temple of my brain
beat the muffled taps of rain . . .

The worm in his retreat deep under
the earth's insipid *crust*
hearing a distant drumming thunder . . .'

Had this been, say, Auden writing, I should have assumed that
the poet's energy had run on ahead of his craftsmanship, and that
he felt it too troublesome to go back and repolish; had it been an even
younger poet, I should have diagnosed that sort of verbal fixation
which causes its sufferer to be, often for weeks, quite incapable of
readjusting his poetic attitude to cope with the sudden technical
problem that his words have produced.

But this is Read's work; it is the work of a man whose poetic
output is small, whose confidence in his tools is great, whose sense
of the appropriate word is almost infallible, and whose feeling for
organic form has been consistent during twenty years. I believe,
then, that Read's honesty forbade him to trick-up a suitable
synonym, or to recast his verse so as to make available more words
from which to choose one that would rhyme with *under*. Honesty
to his impulse prompted the word *crust*, and integrity insisted on its
remaining. There can be no other answer.

Yet another phase of this honesty, this permanence, is visible in
the 'prose' content of Read's poems, where that can be divorced
from the sense of glory, as fundamental of its sort as the mysticism
of Hopkins and the religious devotion of el Greco.

The content of most of the mechanistic poets is derived direct,
often without any show of philosophical transmutation or reduction
'into unity of effect', from the ephemeral manifestations of the
industrial civilisation which is only part of their lives, or from the
matter and manner of an earlier writing, English or Classical, the
permanence of which reassures them. The ballad pastiches of Auden
and Day Lewis, the translations of MacNeice, belong to this argument. Such poetic material may, obviously, be permanent only if the
state of industrialism and the reputations of the original writers be
permanent; the permanence will be a secondhand one, whatever
the case.

But the writer who is strong enough in head and heart to cut
away the decorative or unessential superstructure of the period in
which he lives, who sees fundamentals *with his own eyes*, whose
instrument is unobtrusively functional to his thought and observation—that writer will attain permanence in the truest sense. Such
is the weakness of spirit, the faculty of imitation, the witting or
unwitting whoring after false gods, that only once or twice in a
generation is this achievement possible. And those who seek modish-

ness, mannerism and fashion at the expense of modesty, good manners and permanence must look elsewhere than at the poetry of Herbert Read. They must follow the tinsel, the trumpets and the catchpenny exoticism of those writers whose only burden is a false romanticism, and whose death will take place to the accompaniment of an undignified rush of words to the head.

II

Some years ago, in a review of Read's *Poems 1914–1935*, Michael Roberts wrote words which are worth repeating here:

'The voice is never raised, there is no overstatement, no collapse into a false rhetoric, and there is a curious austerity in the imagery, an absence of harsh contours and strong lights. . . . There is an exultation, the delight of the eye in watching a quick movement without any wish to take part in it. . . . The same detachment appears in the war-poems . . . they show the power to communicate a scene and to imply through the scene itself, the feeling involved, and yet at the same time an intense capacity for sympathy:

"O beautiful men, O men I loved,
O whither are you gone, my company." '

And, to quote Sir Henry Newbolt, whose opinion of Read was always very high, these war-poems contain 'a surgery hardly to be endured'.

In the review already mentioned, Roberts goes on to express the suspicion that Read's poetry is little known, owing to the fact that his other literary activities have given the poems some semblance of being by-products.

Well, the same might be said of Eliot or of Belloc, and I would not believe it in any of these cases. Herbert Read's poems are *known*, if only because of their appearance in every important magazine and anthology; but they are not *popular* for the very reason for which Roberts extols them. They have no overstatement, no false rhetoric, no strong lights and dazzling colours; instead, they have an austerity, a quiet exultation, a detachment, and, above all, 'a surgery hardly to be endured.'

There is yet another reason for Read's poetic 'unfashionableness', a psychological one, bound up with the reader's own shyness and sense of shame, for Read, both in his poetry and in his prose, is remarkably successful in recapturing the mental and emotional states of childhood. He shows you the world as it was to you at the

13

age of nine, before other people came and made you become what you are. There are none of childhood's secrets hidden from him; it is impossible to escape by parading your manhood and blustering:

> 'To the fresh wet fields
> and the white
> froth of flowers
>
> came the wild errant
> swallows with a scream.'
>
> *April*

That is not only what a child must see, but what a child's tongue and mouth do when he is thinking about what he sees. No words of mine can make clearer the insight which enables Read to write:

> 'The farm is distant from the high-road
> half a mile;
>
> The child of the farm
> does not realise it for several years;'
>
> *Childhood*

for if the reader does not come up, with a nostalgic jar, against his own childhood space-fantasies and innocence—then he should not be reading poetry at all.

Still another possible reason for Read's unpopularity may lie in the fact that he has an 'unfair' advantage over most of his readers. He has *been, known, felt* so much; he is too near perfection:

> 'Earth is machine and works to plan,
> Winnowing space and time;
> The ethic mind is engine too,
> Accelerating in the void.'

Let us see what Michael Roberts says about this passage, in *A Critique of Poetry*.

'If we stand in a lift we feel an extra gravitational pull as the lift accelerates upwards. Similarly there would be an apparent gravitational field in a lift accelerating in free space, so that without reference to external landmarks one direction would "feel" different from others. Similarly, as an inevitable consequence of our existence in time, we feel that some acts are good and some are bad, although we perceive no absolute ethical landmarks.

It has taken us seventy words to say what Mr Read said in ten, and even if his writing might seem obscure to some readers, it is entirely unambiguous. He says exactly what he means, and either you understand it or you do not. You cannot misconstrue it.'

As I have said, I believe that piece of writing to be near perfection; so near the sun, in fact, that our eyes are blinded to its poetry, and can only marvel at its incredible exactness, at the mind whose incisive power is such that it can perform so spectacular a feat of cosmic surgery. It is *le mot juste* carried on to a plane where few readers can be expected to follow. It is the very embodiment of the 1913 Imagist Manifesto:

'1. To use the language of common speech, but to employ always the *exact* word, not the merely decorative word.

2. To present an image. We are not a school of painters, but we believe that poetry should render particulars exactly and not deal with vague generalities.

3. To produce poetry that is hard and clear, never blurred or indefinite.

4. We believe that concentration is the very essence of poetry. . . .'

The following two examples from Read's early work (about 1914) will illustrate these points:

'The dark steep roofs chisel
The infinity of the sky:

But the white moonlit gables
Resemble
Still hands at prayer.'   *Night*

Here is the true language of common speech, and how unlike that slipshod jargon which the 'social' novelists and the American tough schools would have us believe as the common medium of expression; *dark, steep, moonlit, prayer.* And could a more exact word than *chisel* have entered any man's head?

If *infinity* is indefinite, so is the concept that it describes: the wideness and the emptiness of the sky are in that word. In the last three lines do we discover Read, the Humanist, in his use of the so personal image (and those who know Dürer's *Hands* will realise the perfection of this image), and in that quiet exultation as he leads us to the spectacle of prayer, to whatever god it may be.

'Shrill green weeds
float on the black pond.
A rising fish
ripples the still water
And disturbs my soul.'   *The Pond*

Once more the Imagist ingredients are there—and notice the pictorial reality of green on black—but this poem is the emotional antithesis of *Night*. The weed is *shrill*, and the soul is *disturbed* by *ripples* which are made by the *rising* fish. Here, in nineteen words, we may learn the distinction between static and dynamic.

And everywhere, in his early and in his most recent work, is apparent a finely controlled equation between form and feeling, head and heart, reason and romanticism. In his *Song for the Spanish Anarchists*, for example, can be observed this equipoise:

> 'The golden lemon is not made
> But grows on a green tree. . .'

says the first verse, with an imagery as pictorially romantic as Marvell's

> '. . . the orange bright
> Like golden lamps in a green night. . . .'

Then

> 'Fifty men own the lemon grove
> and no man is a slave'

says the last lines, and this time it is Read, the Anarchist Philosopher speaking.[1]

And the distinction I would make here between Blake and Read is that while the former's poetry seems to spring direct from his tensions, that, like the above, of Read, is the inevitable residue left when that tension has been resolved by meditation and craftsman control.

In many ways, his war-poems are Read's most amazing productions. They have an infinite compassion, pathos and horror, an utter lack of violence (one of his most marked characteristics), and above all a detachment almost unbelievable in one so physically and mentally implicated in the job of war. (Here I almost wrote 'in the job of killing', until I remembered Read's words in *Annals of Innocence and Experience*: 'During the whole war I never deliberately or consciously killed an individual man . . .')

Observe the horror and the pity of such poems as *The Execution of Cornelius Vane*, the heart-breaking compassion of *My Company*; but observe also the restraint with which the poet shows you what

---

[1] 'The textile industry of Alcoy, the wood industry of Cuenca, the transport system in Barcelona—these are a few examples of the many anarchist collectives which were functioning efficiently for more than two years.'
The Philosophy of Anarchism, H. READ

has moved him so deeply, as in these lines from *The Refugees*, where
the Wordsworthian echo of the last line adds the necessary emotional
overtone which acts as an almost unbearable climax, or foil, to the
tolerable objectivism of the previous lines:

> 'Mute figures with bowed heads
> They travel along the road;
> Old women, incredibly old,
> And a handcart of chattels.
>
> They do not weep:
> *Their eyes are too raw for tears.*'[1]

Again, examine the almost colloquial brevity of this extract from
The Happy Warrior, which, wrote Newbolt, 'in twelve lines of
unerring skill cuts away from fighting all the virtues by which sane
and honourable war survived so long':

> 'His wild heart beats with painful sobs,
> His strained hands clench an ice-cold rifle,
> His aching jaws grip a hot parched tongue,
> His wide eyes search unconsciously.
>
> He cannot shriek.
>
> Bloody saliva
> Dribbles down his shapeless jacket.
>
> I saw him stab
> And stab again
> A well-killed Boche.
>
> This is the happy warrior,
> This is he . . .'

Then, look at the knowledge of men and manners, the quiet
humour which contains more than an element of sadness, inherent
in these lines from *Fear*:

> 'Fear is a wave
> Beating through the air
> And on taut nerves impinging
> Till there it wins
> Vibrating chords.

---

[1] How unfortunate it is that restraint should so often be misunderstood.
'The wilful and cacophonous *pedestrianism* of Herbert Read,' said one
Ronald Fuller, years ago in an article on Tessimond.

All goes well
So long as you tune the instrument
To simulate composure.
  (So you will become
  A gallant gentleman.)'

This is not bitterness, the restraint is everywhere present; nor is it cynicism, its truth is too great for that. 'It is not my business as a poet to condemn war. I only wish to present the universal aspects of a particular event', says Read. The horror of the last verse of the poem quoted above,

'But when the strings are broken,
Then you will grovel on the earth
And your rabbit eyes
Will fill with the fragments of your shattered soul.'

carries with it a condemnation not of war only, but of every other aspect of man's inhumanity to man, be it religious, social or industrial.

As a contrast to this terrifying insight into fear, it would be well to quote from a poem (based on an incident in the story *Ambush*) in which Read shows how, in the midst of war, it is possible by a kindly humour, an intellectual sympathy and a common humanity (sadly enough, too often uncommon in war) to defeat fear, even in circumstances which might be eminently conducive to that emotion, and to become once again, a man. The poem is *Liedholz*:

'When I captured Liedholz
I had a blackened face
Like a nigger's,
And my teeth like white mosaics shone.

We met in the night at half-past one,
Between the lines.
Liedholz shot at me
And I at him;
And in the ensuing tumult he surrendered to me.

Before we reached our wire
He told me he had a wife and three children.
In the dug-out we gave him a whiskey.
Going to the Brigade with my prisoner at dawn,
The early sun made the land delightful,
And larks rose singing from the plain.

18

INTRODUCTION

In broken French we discussed
Beethoven, Nietzsche and the International.

He was a professor
Living at Spandau;
And not too intelligible.

*But my black face and nigger's teeth
Amused him.'*

I have taken the liberty of italicising the lines which, of themselves, show more clearly than anything I can say about them, the restraint, the poetry, the undemonstrative courage, the humour and the kindliness that seem to me so typical of Read, the soldier-poet. And this poem brings to my mind as forcefully as any which he has written, these words by Sir Henry Newbolt: 'Herbert Read is a writer of free-verse with a quality of its own, which recalls the dispassionate wisdom of certain Greek choruses.'

In conclusion, I would comment on the breadth of vision, the tenderness and the sensibility of a poet who can, in one small group of verses, give us a picture of the two young lovers, returning home late on the top of a bus:

> . . . 'their hands linked
> across their laps
> their bodies loosely
> interlocked
>
> their heads resting
> two heavy fruits
> on the plaited
> basket of their limbs . . .
>
> the lovers with
> the hills unfold
>
> wake cold
> to face the fate
> of those who love
> despite the world.' ;

the sensuous beauty of *September Fires,* one of the most perfect lyrical poems of the century,

> 'Haulms burn
> in distant fields.
> Reluctantly the plumes of smoke

rise against a haze
of hills blue and clear
but featureless.

Our feet
crush the crinkled beech-leaves.
There is no other life than ours.
God is good to us this September evening
to give us a sun
and a world burning its dross.

Let us burn the twisted years. . . .'

(*God is good to us this September evening*! The tender humility of the line, the low-voiced gratitude of a man who has been through four years of war for the sake of those qualities which are said to represent God on earth; the pathos of the words is almost unbearable.)

And, finally, the wild, almost despairing splendour of *Cranach*:

'But once upon a time
the oakleaves and the wild boars
Antonio Antonio
the old wound is bleeding . . .'

where, in four brief lines, the superbly chosen allusive and emotive images evoke all the power, the pathos and the magic of the fairy tale, the Ballad, the Provençal Romance and the Elizabethan Tragedy. Here is the passion of parted friends and lovers, the nostalgia of desire, the dull pain of living no less than that of death.

Read once observed that he regarded this poem as a 'test-piece' for the reader of his work. I applaud his use of the term, though I would extend its application to cover the writer no less than the reader, for, whatever the casual reader of poetry may get from this poem, it seems to me certain that the reader who has an adequate background against which to place it, if only of the poetry of the preceding hundred years, will recognise that Read has, in a degree available to few poets, succeeded in passing Eliot's test of the Objective Correlative.

III

' . . I strive
To hold the real design of life
Within the intenser
Light of the mind in these moments.'

The Retreat

I have already quoted Read's words, telling how, by the end of the last war, he had 'made an equation between emotion and image, between feeling and expression'; and that word *equation* is typical of the detached attitude with which he approaches the problems set by his emotions. At the risk of doing him an injustice, I will say that it is the rational or scientific word employed in the description of a romantic feeling or action. It is significant of his whole habit of working, for all the poems are the result of an equation, a balancing, or, to use a common expression whose overtones are more vigorous, a weighing-up—which, in itself, means a sharp scrutiny and a measured consideration. And it is that scrutiny, that consideration, which I would here attempt to describe.

Read has himself told us frequently what it is he wishes to equate, and it is even more than emotion and image, feeling and expression; it is even more than the separable qualities of these emotions and ideas, qualities which may be known as Reason and Romanticism, imagination and realism. 'The very bases of reason, the perceptions of an unclouded intellect, are continually being contradicted by the creative fictions of the imagination, by a world of illusion no less real than the reality of our quick awareness. It is the function of art to reconcile the contradictions inherent in our experience; but obviously an art which keeps to the canons of reason cannot make the necessary synthesis.'[1]

The conflict, in its simplest form, is as well stated in the *Falcon and the Dove*, as anywhere else in Read's poetry:

'This high-caught hooded Reason broods upon my wrist,
Fettered by a so tenuous leash of steel.
We are bound for the myrtle marshes, many leagues away,
And have a fair expectation of quarry.

Over the laggard dove, inclining to green boscage
Hovers this intentional doom—till the unsullied sky receives
A precipitation of shed feathers
And the swifter fall of wounded wings.

Will the plain aye echo with that loud *hullallo*!
Or retain an impress of our passage?
We have caught Beauty in a wild foray
And now the falcon is hooded and comforted away.'

The tension, the conflict, the balance and the conclusion are self-

---

[1] *Annals of Innocence and Experience*, p. 212.

apparent, and I would halt only to comment on the impression we get here that the reason must inevitably be the victor, yet that there is a humane purpose directed to other than the falcon expressed in his adroit hooding—even hoodwinking—and comforting away. And, further, while the poem tells of the reason's triumph, the language it uses is a tribute to romanticism, as in such words as *fettered, leagues, laggard, boscage, foray*.[1] And, perhaps most interesting of all, the very instrument of Reason, the falcon, is a medieval, and hence Romantic, object! There lies a tension within a tension, and the final solution of the poem—though not of the problem, for that is never-ending—is as balanced, as equated, as is the Chinese puzzle-box, where element emerges from element, it seems indefinitely, until out of the reduplicative chaos rises a perfect and symmetrical pyramid.

This then is one of the problems with which Read is concerned; one of the designs which, one day if he is spared, he hopes to hold within the intenser light of the mind; not only in the poems, but in the prose, critical and philosophical. Seen even more clearly in its elemental form, it is the problem of *Cranach*, from which I have previously quoted only the first verse:

'But once upon a time
the oakleaves and the wild boars
Antonio Antonio
the old wound is bleeding.

We are in Silvertown
we have come here with a modest ambition
to know a little bit about the river
eating cheese and pickled onions on a terrace by the Thames.

Sweet Thames! the ferry glides across your bosom
like Leda's swan.
The factories ah slender graces
sly naked damsels nodding their downy plumes.'

where, after the essentially romantic first section, we are presented with a thoroughly realist second verse, followed by a third

[1] For those who have not considered this point, the distribution of romantic and scientific words in Read's vocabulary is enlightening. The following examples are taken almost at random from the poems: ROMANTIC: lanthorn, plumes, shrived, leafy, pillag'd, ere, coign, tresses. SCIENTIFIC: diatoms, console, equable, atavistic, sodality, perceptual.

section in which the realist elements are described in romantic language.[1]

This battle in its fundamental form can be as well fought out within the compass of a short lyric as in a poem of epic length, yet there are other conflicts in Read's mind which need a larger battleground, where many sections may manœuvre independently, it seems, of each other, to attack the common enemy, their unity of purpose visible only to the detached observer who can look upon the conflict from afar.

Such battlegrounds are the long poems, 'Beata l'Alma', 'Mutations of the Phoenix', and 'The Analysis of Love'; and the causes

[1] It has been suggested to me that this abrupt change of tone is perhaps due to the influence of T. S. Eliot; Read's own words in *Annals of Innocence and Experience* probably support this view. 'These friendships (with Flint, Aldington, Pound, Eliot) no doubt modified my poetic outlook. . . .' It may be worth noticing that T. S. Eliot, in the third section of *The Waste Land*, not only uses the Thames as a poetic subject, but roughly the same reach of the river as Read's, Greenwich Reach: and, furthermore, that he attacks his own romantic-realist problem with the identical words from Spenser which Read employs:

'Sweet Thames, run softly till I end my song . . .'

A more puzzling point of influence (though that is almost surely too strong a word here) occurs in Read's *A Short Poem for Armistice Day*:

'. . . work it diverse ways
work it diverse days . . .'

Eliot has a similar construction in *Journey of the Magi*:

'. . . but set down
this set down
This . . .'

Which he has taken from *Othello*:

' . . . Set you down this;
And say, besides, that in Aleppo once . . .'

A more obvious point of contact between the two writers may be seen in the following extracts:

'Between the Winter and the Spring
between day and night
a no man's time a mean light . . .'

Inbetweentimes, READ

'Between the idea
And the reality
Between the motion
And the act
Falls the Shadow'

The Hollow Men, ELIOT

which are fought out on these fields, while perhaps superficially distinct, are really phases of that one unifying desire, 'to hold the real design of life within the intenser light of the mind.'

In 'The Seven Sleepers', the poet says:

> 'Beauty when we wake will be
> a solitude on land and sea.'

and so expresses a desire (as sincere as that of Yeats, and less theatrically expressed) for peace of the body—a recurrent idea— the gentle ranging of the mind in a heaven somewhere between fancy and reality, reason and emotion. It is a strangely clear, hard conception of Beauty (or perfection), almost clean to the point of aridity. It is, I believe, that form of Nirvana which Read has symbolised by The Tree of Life.

I mention this because in 'Beata l'Alma', after a reference to the seven sleepers, Read seems to develop this desire as well as the conflicts which are entailed in its acquisition. The world, as he feels it (I dare not think that he *sees* it so), is almost the nightmare of the Canterbury Women before the murder of the Archbishop; it is a place of terror and disgust, the very obverse of the beautiful world that the sleepers hope to find, where

> '. . . men are ghoulish stumps
> and the air a river of opaque
> filth.'

(And for me there is infinitely more to be loathed in the stumps than in the filth, for I am reminded of a personal horror of mutilation: the other can, presumably, be put right by the miracles of modern science, which, we are told, operate about us every minute of the day.)

There, then, is another sort of tension stated immediately, and the next stage in the battle shows the poet's humble desire to light such a lantern as will show men the truth, as will bring them to a clean world of healing and salvation.

But this wish is just as immediately countered by the poet's painful and swift recollection that man does not want to be saved, to be healed, that he is by his very nature a materialistic cynic:

> '. . . No fellows
> would answer my hullallo,'

he says in a quiet despair.

But the fight is not yet over. There must be hope for the future! Surely, there shall come a time when the world is inhabited by a race of Gods, doomed to no mortal death and disease, freed from the yoke of lying words and of love that turns to hate, with no flaw of mind or of flesh.

Then once again the balance swings; the poet is aware of his idealism, his romanticism, and he has knowledge of the vulnerability of his argument. So, as the poem moves to its close, he makes the only equation possible to himself as a man without foreknowledge; he asserts that the divine state is, at least, a possibility; for

'. . . Art ends;
the individual world alone is valid.'

The inquiry is carried a stage further in 'Mutations of the Phoenix', a poem which, if not his greatest, is surely on a level which only the finest of poetic minds may attain.

Once more, as in the two poems already mentioned, there is expressed the desire that all things should be cleanly perfect, that the world should be washed of the commonness of humanity:

'Our limbs
settle into the crumbling sand.
There will be our impress here
until the flowing tide
erases
all designs the fretful day leaves here.'

He sees the same flame which is to cleanse the world cleansing mankind, and he says:

'The one flame
burns many phenomena.'[1]

Then, by contrast with the hard philosophy of the preceding lines, there follows a splendid passage of *poetic* reasoning:

'Does a white flame
burn among the waves?

Will a phoenix arise
from a womb evolved

---

[1] The flame, or fire, the act of burning, is a constantly recurring symbol in Read's poetry:

' . . . The white flame of justice
will dance wildly over Europe's dark marshes

 (*note continued on p. 26.*)

among the curved crests of foam?
At Aphrodite's birth
were the waters in white flame?'

But this mood may not be sustained in one whose apprehensions are as multiple as Read's are. Uncertainty intervenes, and this time the simple solution of 'Beata l'Alma' is discredited:

'Why should I dwell in individual ecstasy?'

almost groans the sufferer.[1]

How, then, is one to look at the world? Is it perhaps possible to see it with the eye alone, even though one despises the

---

until the morning air is everywhere
and clear
as on the hills of Hellas.'   *Herschel Grynsban*

Let us burn the twisted years
that have brought us to this meeting'   *September Fires*

'The limbs remember fire and joy,'   *Time Regained*

'Against the anguish of the herbal flames'
                                               Formal Incantation

' . . . the lusts
that burnt us were
too sweet.'   *The Complaint of Heloise*

' . . . the voice of the yellow sunflowers
pouring fire into the dusk.'   *Hulk*

Where fire is not descriptive, or is simply symbolic of lust, I imagine that it refers to the preliminary to Godhead, to be an element of faith in a future state of perfection; the same faith which makes Read an anarchist, the belief that man is inherently good, that given the right opportunities he will find and prove the goodness in himself; for, as he says in *To Hell with Culture*: 'we see that certain proportions in nature . . . are right, and we carry over these proportions into the things we make—not deliberately, but instinctively.'

It is that instinctive ability to see the *rightness* of things—called the conscience when it operates in the direction of actions—which will make men into Gods one day, perhaps, but before that day they will have to go through the fire, the flame.

[1] 'When your life is most real, to me you are mad; when your agony is blackest, I look at you and wonder. Friendship is good, a strong stick; but when the hour comes to lean hard, it gives. In the day of their bitterest need all souls are alone.'   *The Story of an African Farm*

'Greedy eye wanting things finite'?[1]
No, the finite eye is not enough; alone, it may not see the truth.
It must be assisted by the mind, for

> 'Effort of consciousness
> carries from origin
> the metamorphic clue.'

Also must the conscience be engaged:

> 'Conscience is control, ordaining the strain
> to some perfection
> not briefly known.'

Then, once more, follows a revulsion from the world of men, men who must maul everything with their eyes, who cannot progress beyond mere physical vision. There is here a stiffening of the poet's attitude, almost an arrogant sharpness, as though he is at the same moment conscious not only of his mission to teach, but also of the Godhead within himself, the power of vision, which enables him to do so.

> 'We must not be oversubtle with these fools
> else we defeat ourselves, not urging them.'

And again, just as inevitably, there is another swing of the balance towards pity, remorse, and a knowledge of the inescapable failure which he shares with all men:

> 'You can't escape: don't escape
> poor easeless human mind.
> Better leave things finite.'

Yet there is a sort of escape for the poet himself, perhaps, one day, for all men. It lies in the magnificent vision of the phoenix as the life-spirit, the transcendental conception of glory, the spark of human greatness leading to Godhead. While it lives, the whole universe can be seen for what it is, and the shackles of earthly sight thrown off.

[1] Read quotes Bergson, one of his influences, as saying: 'Our eye perceives the features of the living being, merely as assembled, not as mutually organised. The intention of life, the simple movement that runs through the lines, that binds them together and gives them significance, escapes it. This intention is just what the artist tries to regain, in placing himself back within the object by a kind of sympathy, in breaking down, by an effort of intuition, the barrier that space puts up between him and his model.'
Annals of Innocence and Experience, page 191

But once it is dead, all that is left is the eye:

'The eye is all: is hierarch of the finite world.
Eye gone light gone, and the unknown is very near.'

And so this poem ends, having shown, once more, the conflict: having given, if only to take it away again immediately, the taste of victory. For this divine bird is the fiery energy that carries men on to war with the world of mere things, the vulgar mechanistic world. Though man is, after all, but humanly frail as yet: his bodily clay must crack in the fierce flame of his spirit—so he must rest. The sacred phoenix must die if the flesh is to have ease.

Yet the flesh will become whole again, the phoenix will be reborn —and the struggle will inevitably start again. Once more will the poet strive to hold the real design of life within the intenser light of the mind. Nor may he ever achieve full vision, the victory, the balanced equation, until he achieves also godlike perfection.

Until then he will be capable only of stating the problem, which is not his alone, but the world's, could the world understand that it is so.

'The Analysis of Love' presents us with one more conflict in search of an equation; another facet of the same great problem, located on another plane of experience.

First comes the stated desire for a total apprehension, not a mere personal one, but one which may be shared with all men, and seen as truth:

'I would have my vision
The world's vision'

But sadly, there are so many concepts which the solitary mind can grasp, but which it is incapable of transmitting to others (a fairly common idea in Read's metaphysical poetry, the finite bounds of the infinite mind) and if these things could ever be told, the world would stop turning and the end of all would come.

The poet now proceeds to struggle towards some understanding of the nature of love, himself, and himself in love.

Night is powerful to ease the mind of its lusts, but sleep is all-powerful. (Once again, the *ease* motif. 'I have been half in love with easeful death', said Keats so similarly, though he would have been incapable of following Read's scientific movement forward to describe sleep as having 'its cone of annihilation', a remarkably just image.) Lust is finite and physical, therefore may its magnitude be measured by the mind, which is capable of understanding all finite things. But the appeal of love is infinite, and so is without any hope of finite measurement and comprehension.

But are there not moments, brief spaces of intuitive grasp, when it is possible to define the limits and the nature of love?

No, that is a mere illusion. Man himself is physical, finite, and may not hold the infinite within his mind. And that is the only reason why lovers should ever despair—not that their love has shown a frailty which, in the end, is but to be expected, but that they are of their very nature incapable of defining the passion which is so moving their thoughts and their actions.

But, though reason itself is powerless to measure an emotion, surely the struggles of all men to understand must ultimately result in some progress towards understanding? Or is the concept of *understanding* itself an illusion? Is there, perhaps, nothing to understand?

Yet we must hope, despite our knowledge of human weaknesses, that there is possible to us, in another world than this, a higher state of being and understanding, a movement towards divinity, perfectness. Even though all we are sure of now is that suffering is inevitable on earth, and just as inevitable is the decay of our zest for love.

Here, as in the other poems, is that desire for complete understanding, the same hope for perfection, and the same alternation of despair and aspiration. And, as before, we are left with a brave injunction to endeavour, without which man can never reach the highest point of development.

There may be, as Read says, an equation between his emotions and the words which he uses to express them, though it would seem humanly inevitable that the higher form of equation which he seeks, between emotion and emotion, or concept and concept, may never be accomplished. We can only hope with him that by his struggle he will prepare himself, and us, for a conception of transcendental reality which is at the moment outside the human grasp.

In 'The Retreat', he not only recognises the problems there are to be faced, but, it seems, resigns himself to a less exalted solution than that of Godhead:

> 'Life
> Is but one mechanism more to manifest the force
> Active even in the gulfs of uncreated space.'

and

> 'Beyond time and space there is a beauty
> Not to be seized by men in prison, who but languish

29

In shackles carried from the womb, and worn
Unto the release of death: unto the dark return
Of the world's harmony.'[1]

I would add that a mark of Read's magnitude as a poet is his grasp as a philosopher, for the poet must be something more than a mere spinner of words if he is to take his place in the final hierarchy. That Read is unable to present us with a certain solution—the function of the philosopher as philosopher, and not of the poet as philosopher—is but a reminder that he has not yet acquired divine status; that he is able to present us with the problems themselves at all is not only a fine *tour de force* of the poet, but an achievement of the teacher.

And, lest there should be any who doubt the powers of Read's personal philosophy to heal and to comfort, I would, in conclusion, present the stoic acceptance, the self-renunciation, and the Taoist tranquillity of 'Time Regained':

> 'The limbs remember blood and fire:
> a hurt that's done may in the mind
> sink and lose identity;
>
> for the mind has reasons of its own
> for covering with an eyeless mask
> marks of mortality.
>
> The limbs remember fire and joy
> and flesh to flesh is benison
> of entity;
>
> but the mind has reasons of its own
> for circumventing life and love's
> sodality.'[2]

As I have said, the failure is not surprising: the achievement is remarkable.

---

[1] 'They say that in the world to come time is not measured out by months and years. Neither is it here. The soul's life has seasons of its own; periods not found in any calendar, times that years and months will not scan, but which are as deftly and sharply cut off from one another as the smoothly-arranged years which the earth's motion yields us.'
The Story of an African Farm

[2] 'The troubles of the young are soon over; they leave no external mark. If you wound the tree in its youth the bark will quickly cover the gash; but when the tree is very old, peeling the bark off, and looking carefully, you will see the scar there still. All that is buried is not dead.'
The Story of an African Farm

IV

No essay on the poetry of Herbert Read can be in any way adequate which does not at least consider the general formal theory that underlies some of his longer poems.

Some time ago Herbert Read said, 'They are an attempt to do something which is extremely difficult and yet not to be shirked. . . . They constitute a search for a form for the long poem which is not merely a continuation of the same kind of thing more or less indefinitely (blank verse, rhymed couplets, etc.), or an addition of identical units (a sonnet sequence), but a poem on the analogy of *the Quartet in music*, with separate movements, forms within the form, diversity within unity. . . .'

I would say that, quite obviously, Read is not practising this theory in many of his longer poems, in 'The Analysis of Love', 'Beata l'alma', or even 'Mutations of the Phoenix', in all of which cases there seems to be an insistence on the short stanza form. Yet, in 'The Lament of Saint Denis', 'The Nuncio', and especially in 'The End of a War', the musical analogy is almost immediately apparent.[1]

And it is 'The End of a War' about which I would like particularly to speak here. It is a poem of about eighteen pages, divided into three sections, with a preceding 'Argument', a piece of dignified prose, noble and complete in its own rights, the annotated programme which tells us what to look for as the work proceeds, heightening the effects of the 'music' perhaps by its own objective terseness. This 'Argument' tells how, on Nov. 10, 1918, some British soldiers were betrayed by a badly wounded German officer into entering a fortified village, where over a hundred of them were killed before they succeeded in capturing the stronghold. A corporal returned to bayonet the German, 'who seemed to be expecting him, his face did not flinch as the bayonet descended.' Meanwhile, the British discovered the mutilated body of a young French girl, but their officer, seeing that nothing could now be done, sank into an exhausted sleep, and did not wake until the next day, Nov. 11, 1918.

[1] When I commented to Read that I saw the same motives apparent in Pound's *Hugh Selwyn Mauberley*, in Eliot's *Waste Land* and *The Hollow Men*, with their motifs and changing tempos, and that it seemed to me the end of such experiment would always be drama (as in *Murder in the Cathedral*), he replied that this theory was 'a substitute for drama, for that poetic stand which no longer has any real function in the community.'

This, then, is the background explanation of the circumstances which inspired the poem.

The poem itself does not retell the story, but in the forms of dialogue or meditation, isolates from the narrative those emotional and philosophical focal-points which share something of music's abstract qualities, maintaining the illusion of the Quartet, in which each poetic section represents a musical Movement, and each idea, or sequence of ideas, a musical theme or motif.

The first Movement ('Meditation of the Dying German Officer') has a quiet strength and purpose, displaying what had been seen as cruelty and double-dealing on a plane where they cease to be reprehensible. There is even a high moral purpose in his treachery, and a magnificent stoicism in his poetic renunciation of the world which the corporal's bayonet steals from him:

> '. . . Now Chaos intervenes
> and I leave not gladly but with harsh disdain
> a world too strong in folly for the bliss of dreams.'

It is humanly impossible to condemn the pride with which this man speaks of his Fatherland:

> 'This is a tangible trust. To make it secure
> against the tempests of inferior minds
> to build it in our blood, to make our lives
> a tribute to its beauty—there is no higher aim.'

The tempo is everywhere slow and unhurried; the motifs clear, balanced and compassionate.

'His face did not flinch as the bayonet descended.' There is no ritenuto, only a measured and dignified diminuendo, enforced by sharp steel.

'I die, but death was destined,' says the German as he looks up into the corporal's angry face.

The second Movement ('Dialogue between the Body and the Soul of the Murdered Girl'), piquant as a duet for oboe and viola, is in strong contrast to the first section; it is a two-part invention, with soul and body as its voices, whose speeds are varied; moving at the different paces of objective narrative, philosophy and emotional experience.

Only where the speed is greatest does the volume increase, as in the passage:

> 'SOUL: The mind grew tense.
> BODY: My flesh was caught
>   in the cog and gear of hate.

SOUL: I lay coiled, the spring
    of all your intricate design.
BODY: You served me well. But still I swear
    Christ was my only King.'[1]

Elsewhere, the sad pitying voices are not raised. A deed has been done which can never be undone. Both soul and body are aware of the crime's finality, of the futility of grief and theatrical despair.

It is therefore a source of some sadness to me that Read should close this Movement with the lines:

'Those who die for a cause die comforted and coy;
   believing their cause God's cause they die with joy.'

where the strength of the concept is dissipated by the banality forced on the poet by his choice of the couplet; a banality which, let it be said, Read would be one of the first, and most convincing, to defend.

After the dying German and the mutilated girl, the waking English officer seems like a child in his simpleness, and the Movement which is his Meditation seems to proceed at a child's irregular and arbitrary pace, now hopping, now loitering, now almost standing stock-still, but always moved by that ecstasy which Richard Church noticed in the poem.

'Look: I am alive, alive, alive!'

shouts the young man's heart as he wakes to find that the hell of war has passed and left his body unbroken; and there is all childhood in that 'Look!' It is the child, delirious almost with happiness, who would open the eyes of the dull grown-ups to a recognition of his new treasure. The repetition of 'alive' is the sobbing thankfulness that comes with the passing of the nightmare, when the room is filled once more by the bright clean spirit of daytime, the kindly, known things that are the child's armour against the things of darkness.

This poem in general, and this section in particular, could be read at no more poignant time than this, when thousands of young men are being flung into the nightmare from which the young officer is so thankful to have escaped whole. At any time, this is a splendid poem: today, its dramatic irony makes it a great one.

---

[1] I would like those who condemn Read's 'sense of glory' as a mere substitute for religion, and Read himself for his words in *The Philosophy of Anarchism*, 'I have no religion to recommend and none to believe in,' to consider the pure religious feeling of this section, as saintly a piece of writing as it is possible to imagine.

This, then, is the final Movement of the 'Quartet', and, to preserve the balance of the whole work, it ends appropriately in the major. There is more than acceptance in the *piano* with which it concludes; there is once more that exultation which I noticed earlier in this essay:

> 'in light celestial
> infinite and still
> eternal
> bright.'

The poised words, the retardation of the last two lines, as dignified and composed as an Easter Week procession in Notre Dame de Paris, are as close as we shall ever get in words to that sweet fall which closes a perfectly worked-out musical idea, in the course which the composer has passed through all the tones and tempests of his experience, pointing and counter-pointing his emotional motifs, producing his climax, the hope of maturity hewn from the peaks and chasms of his feeling.

There is a kind, compassionate *tierce de Picardie*, then peace: the stillness that follows the Beethoven Ninth in the seconds before applause sets the air rocking.

That such a poem as 'The End of a War', because of its ambition, its attempts to transcend an established medium, should have its faults cannot be denied.

To my mind, such phrases as:
'banned from Heaven by light electric',
'the world's pallid sphere',
'I filled your vacant ventricles with dreams'
do not ring quite true; that is, they do not seem the valid experience of the poet who could write 'April' and 'Cranach'.

Nor am I able, with any comfort, to adjust my reactions in time to such abrupt transitions from sublimity as:

> 'The bells of hell ring ting a ling
> For you but not for me . . .'

which may be good 'character' as spoken by the English officer, but which is not of a piece with that detachment which causes Read to quote before his poem:

> 'Today it is from afar that we look at life, death is
> near us, and perhaps nearer still is eternity.'

Yet such personal maladjustments come near to being impertinence when the sheer magnitude of the poem is contemplated; a remarkable philosophical, almost mystic experiment; the distillation into a work of art of all wartime experience; the intellectual and emotional landmark which stands at the end of a war, and which, in a sane world, would stand for the end of all wars.

No, Herbert Read can never be a 'popular' poet in the sense that Auden has been a popular poet, and in the sense that Hemingway has been a popular novelist. He will not do the parlour-tricks; he will not tell his readers just the sort of thing they want to be told for comfort's sake. He draws his morals deeper down than the ruined pitshaft goes, from those flashes of naked insight that are tougher than anything the gangster can think up, because they are the quintessence of *all* suffering and *all* strength.

If all his poems were on the level of that comic one that yells:

> 'Yarrol! Yarrol! I cried exultingly:
> Passing dogs lifted wet noses
> And housemaidens the blinds of their gables.'

things might be different.

It is a dispensation of some sort of providence that Read is also a philosopher, who can say dispassionately—though endeavouring by this statement[1] to remedy such a state: 'Poetry, at any rate under the present economic dispensation, is dead letters. Poetry is ceasing to be printed; poetry is no longer read.' And earlier still: 'All art, as Wilde said, is entirely useless. Conceivably my poetry makes life tolerable to me, and there are a few, a very few, people who find enjoyment in it.'[2]

V

In discussing a writer whose many activities are as closely correlated as Read's are, it is nearly impossible to avoid some measure of overlapping if anything like a rounded impression is to be given; I hope therefore that the other contributors to this volume will pardon my stepping, though so lightly, on to their preserves for a few moments.

Read's prose has for me in general most of the qualities that I have observed in his verse, with none of that diffuseness which is often the main distinction between a man's poems and his prose. His philosophy and his criticism have a naturalness, a satisfying

---

[1] *New Verse.* Autumn 1938. 'An Open Letter to the B.B.C.' asking for radio readings of poetry.

[2] *New Verse.* Answers to an Enquiry. Oct. 1934.

solidity and a breadth which bring to mind once more those words on the laws of nature: 'Rhythm, proportion, balance, precision, economy. . . .' Read's prose has all these attributes. And, what is more, it has a versatile validity which makes it the only adequate instrument for his diverse departures; it is general utility prose of the highest order, clear, sensitive, restrained, moving quietly and without theatrical impediment to evoke character, scene, incident or reasoning, inevitably and delightfully. It is as at-home in the cowshed;

'The warm needle stream of milk hissed into the gleaming pails. At first it sang against the hollow tin drum of the base, but as the pail filled it murmured with a frothy *surr-surr* . . .'

as in the lecture-room:

'A personality . . . is distinguished by immediacy, by what I would call lability, or the capacity to change without loss of integrity . . . and in Hamlet, Shakespeare depicted the type in all its mutability. . . . Character is only attained by limitation.'

Where else, in the body of one man's work might one find a statement on Picasso (—and on art beyond Picasso) which has the *cogency* of:

'After creating abstract art, the pure techtonics of form and colour, he moved to the opposite pole and created *surréalisme*, a form of art that denies art, that seeks only the naked heart, the unknown, the uncreated, the dreaded Minotaur in the dark labyrinth of the unconscious mind. . . . His faith is, that what he creates out of love, and with passion, will be found beautiful. . . . It is a dangerous creed, opening the realm of art to all kinds of charlatans, who can claim that their confusion is inspiration, their chaos a unity worthy of our consideration. But I do not know whether more charlatans can shelter under such a doctrine than gather under the classical porticos of academic competence. Mediocrity is no more tolerable for being tidy.'

the *tolerance* of his remarks on Toulouse-Lautrec:

'he came out into the world, but chiefly into the underworld. A sense of his physical oddness may have driven him there, but he found it much to his taste. . . . But this he did in a mood not precisely immoral or immodest. This was his chosen milieu, where he found a certain aspect of life, a certain gaiety and lack of affectation, all of which appealed to his spirit.'

the *technical wisdom of*:

'Klee recognises in painting only the essential categories—line, colour and surface—and he does not hesitate to employ any conceivable means to produce effects of line, colour and surface. That is to say, a neat division like "oil-painting" is arbitrary and unnecessary; if it suits the artistic purpose, why not mix the mediums and reverse the processes, paint with oils on paper and with water colours on canvas, or with a mixture of both on gesso? So long as the resulting effect is an artistic one, there is no reason beyond a timid academic tradition why the work 'of art should not be produced by any material the artist can find to produce the effect he requires. That some of his experiments may not stand the test of time is probably true, but what medium is wholly exempt from that form of destruction?'

or the *exactness* of his assessment of Patmore:

'This intellectual arrogance represents a certain settling of his fluent feminine personality, the psychological condition of his poetic force, along firm lines of masculine character inhibitive to this force, and there can be little doubt that this tendency was immensely accelerated by the decision he had to make about this time—he had not only to compromise in some degree with his doctrine of the inviolability of nuptial love, but concurrently was impelled by his conscience to make the final act of submission and become a member of the Catholic Church.'

Over all is Read's balance, his mellow labile judgment, his courage and sense of reality. He is a true teacher, whose opinions must always command respect, if not always compliance, because of their so obvious sincerity and organic existence as fundamental growths from a live mind.

Whether one is or is not an imperialist makes no difference to the recognition of the truth of a passage such as this:

'It may be true that we do not want any more colonies or to extend our empire in any way; but we mean to defend what we have got, which is an unfair share, and between such defence and aggression there is no essential difference.'

And here is the perfect common-sense answer to those Marxist literary critics who, a few years ago, found their pleasure in equating the creative impulses of Ben Jonson and Shakespeare with their own political tenets:

'Chaucer, Malory and Shakespeare do not survive because they were on the progressive side of the class-struggle, nor even because they made good reports of the contemporary events. They survive because they were able to transform their experience into the finer and remoter element we call poetry.'

It all looks so easy—'I do not think it will be necessary for a reader of the future to approach my work with squared shoulders' —like the well-oiled movement of a slow bowler, or a light-weight boxer. It is only when one tries to do the trick oneself that its difficulty is realised, and the skill which brought these ideas into the external world appreciated.'

Yet it is easy, fatally easy, to continue in this way, reprinting passages from Read, with occasional comments of my own, to justify my presence, so to speak. If, on this occasion, my attitude needs a defence, this shall be my answer: to attempt a pre-digested exposition of Herbert Read's theories and style would be the most arrant impertinence. I would rather present the substance than the shadow, which I do, with the fullest confidence in the world that there is no man who can explain himself so interestingly and so adequately as can Herbert Read.

VI

For me, the ultimate attraction of Read's work, and of his character, for the two must always be mentioned together, lies in enigma, paradox, and perfectly wedded opposites. It is nothing as simple as 'Poet or Critic?', 'Artist or Philosopher?'. It is more nearly the 'Marriage of Heaven and Hell'; it is more nearly still a complete recognition and absorption of the totality of experience, psycho-physical, emotional and intellectual. Such a recognition and absorption as must inevitably produce the theory of lability; poems, prose, criticism and political theory. Such a wholeness as must inevitably produce within one mind, and within one body of work, strength and delicacy, permanence and lyricism, tolerance and clarity, reason and romanticism, fervour and balance, maturity and enthusiasm. Honesty at innumerable points, a form of multiple integrity, a final anarchic sanity; the philosophical code of every adult man who has let his eyes wander over the face of the world, and his mind ponder over what they have seen. And the thing that always stupefies me at this point is, that Read, who is representative of more phases of human recognition than any other writer living today, can externalise those phases with complete clarity and sincerity, so that the image is never blurred, the language never misused, the high standard of selection never impaired.

INTRODUCTION

It can only be that he has succeeded where so many have failed, withal the loud voice and the superficial brilliance which he eschews, in obeying to a degree previously unattainable those primary laws of nature, which he calls physical—rhythm, proportion, balance, precision, economy. . . .

That he has his faults, however, must be accepted, as we accept the fact that he is a very distinguished artist; and one may find faults according to the canons of one's times and milieu, in any other distinguished artist—in Marlowe, Webster, Donne, Blake, Van Gogh, yes, even Shakespeare—for, where there are no faults perfection loses its value, its very existence.

The poet, for example, may argue that Read has invented no spectacularly original 'form', that he has lagged behind Hopkins or even Meredith, forgetting that there is a form which is greater, more organic, than any 'form', a poetic return to the previously mentioned 'laws of nature', laws which are so wide, even so subterranean, in their operation, as to be invisible to all but the sharpest eye and the most fully informed perception. The poet might object that the poetic *surgery* has been overdone, that to cut down to the bone of a poem is an act of cruelty rather than one of artistry. He might cite, as clinical exhibits, such poems as 'Melville':

'Melville fell
and the albatross
out of the rigging

Edam the moon
all angular else
mast and ropes

a feather fell
a claw
clutched the ladder

slipped
Melville fell
forty fathoms Melville fell

fathoms below the sea level.'

or 'Flight':

'The serial feathers
imbricated
conceal the struts

an extending
N: flexed;
when taut

folding air
coiling the currents
never bending

till the body
seeks the level
of its rest.'

ignoring the fact that such poems form a very small portion of Read's work, ignoring their effect, as salutary as that of T. S. Eliot, in helping to stay the epidemic of Georgianism and Hopkinsitis, ignoring their function by implication (which exists alongside their permanent artistic *entity*) as a physic for all lavish rankness.[1]

The art-critic might accuse Read of a different sort of fault; that of following too many gods, that of being only too ready to fling himself into the fight for an attractive idea. But such a critic would be denying Read his very nature, his lability, his tolerance and breadth, overlooking that generous vitality which they are too self-conscious to display in public, or even to possess in private. Such a critic would miss the whole point of Read's words on another poet, words which can so easily and so truly be applied to his own case: 'He is humble before the elemental tragedy of life.' For Read's humility is only the obverse of his honest solidity; it is the humility of the man who can recognise, probe and still respect the multiplicity of the world in which he walks; that of the man who knows, for all his individual complexity, that he is but one fragment, one element in a vast compound, one minute charge of electricity that helps to form a small particle of matter, which, multifold, is mankind.

[1] *The Literary Review*, noticing Michael Roberts' poems in 1936, said, with what I believe to be justice: 'He reverences T. E. Hulme, but does not imitate him. If any influence is obvious it is that of Herbert Read in style.'

I fancy that Dylan Thomas' 'Light breaks', has grown from the germ which is contained in the last line of Read's 'Logos':

'and light breaks in behind the brain.'

Many other examples of the influence which Read has had over the younger poets might be named, but the most obvious ones will be found in the early work of Cecil Day Lewis and in the first two books of Clifford Dyment, *First Day* and *Straight or Curly?*

Therefore, I admire the brave humility with which he lends his name to the small magazines; for the Quixote in him that writes prefaces to Limited editions; for the kindliness with which he encourages the young artists (often as dangerous an act as that of petting a baby alligator!).

Above all, I respect the cordiality and forbearance which allows him to reply to an importunate critic in these words:

'In the past two or three years, Mr Hugh Gordon Porteus has pursued me with an analytical criticism which I take in the best possible part. Though I think at times he has misrepresented me, the fault may have been mine, because I am conscious that occasionally, for the sake of a fine phrase, or an effective generalisation, I am apt to jump at an idea which I have not carefully related to what is fundamental in my theories. But, in any case, I do not pose as a system-maker; even my ideas are given their configuration by aesthetic impulses, and like the true romantic that I am, I do not hesitate to follow the logic of the imagination in preference to that of the understanding.'

Read himself once said of Picasso: 'Here is a genius too violent to be constrained within the categories of one art.' I would substitute *fertile* for *violent*, and apply the remark to Read himself, for only thus could one pay adequate tribute to such versatility as he has shown during the last twenty years. A versatility which I cannot hope alone to reflect in this small essay; which I cannot even hope to appreciate for many years to come, perhaps never, but which, here in this book, we are all attempting to suggest rather than explain, so that while we still have him, and more important, while we still need him, we may understand if ever so slightly, some of those qualities which must earn Herbert Read a high place in the literary hierarchy of the century.

I will end this essay with some words by Janet Adam Smith, who, within the limits of her brevity, has paid Read one of the highest compliments a poet can receive:

'The richness and profundity of the Bible is largely in this quality of constantly surprising us by a new shade, a new significance; and the reason I, at any rate, find poems of Herbert Read . . . so satisfying is that they seem to show a greater wisdom, a deeper feeling, and a wider experience at the fifth reading than at the first.'

E. H. RAMSDEN

HERBERT READ'S PHILOSOPHY OF ART

Criticism, as Pope observed, is an invidious task: for while it requires for its practice taste, judgement, learning, candour and truth, and the exercise of a genius second only to that of the poet, it carries with it a greater probability of error than any other theoretical activity of comparable distinction. For unlike a scientific hypothesis or a mathematical proposition, an aesthetic judgement is incapable of proof and can never therefore be conclusive in the same way. But this does not invalidate the principles on which it is based, nor does it lessen the importance of the critical faculty which is not only allied to the creative, but, as such, to that which Giambattista Vico, the founder of modern aesthetics, regarded as primitive and fundamental—the power of imaginative expression. On the contrary, if, as Croce contends in his exposition and development of this theory, the creative and critical faculties differ not in kind but only in degree, it may even be said that the very fallibility of the judgement is a proof that it belongs, like other vital and formative processes, to the perpetual 'becoming' of life, of which finality, in one sense, must always be a negation. Moreover, in so far as the exact sciences are tending increasingly towards the acceptance of 'the principle of indeterminacy', the fact that aesthetics must likewise be 'satisfied with probabilities' may be regarded as significant.

If, then, the theory of art is progressive, no judgement of taste can be absolute, though it may remain true within the limits of its statement, which is perhaps the most that can be required of it— as of the critic, who must, nevertheless, be held responsible for his opinions, whether they be valid or otherwise. At the same time, when he has once determined the principles of his aesthetic creed he cannot be expected to justify his conclusions, since 'what is wrong with criticism today', as Herbert Read, himself, has pointed out, 'is not too much dogma, but too little'—a statement that is not only true on the face of it, but one which indicates that criticism is no enviable task nor lightly to be undertaken.

Thus, in the preface to the first edition of *Art Now* Read sets forth the view that 'Positive criticism begins as an impulse to defend one's preferences; but it only deserves the name of criticism if it reaches beyond the personal standpoint to one that is universal'. From this it follows that the greatness of a critic (his possession of the natural endowments, intuition, a profound understanding and the ability to communicate his experience being assumed) will always be in proportion to the impartiality of his judgement and in the degree to which he is able to exclude the personal element without violating his deeper susceptibilities. To this extent his conclusions will tend to be correct. But while it is true that the complete elimination of prejudice is possible only in theory, its acceptance in principle is vital to a just estimation of work to which the critic as an *individual* may happen to be less rather than more responsive. For although it is one thing to experience a work of art emotionally and another to admit its perfections, the nature of human genius is such that as between two works of equal and unquestionable merit, some allowance must be made for personal choice, notwithstanding the utmost intellectual detachment on the critic's part. Also, if it is true that 'what intuition reveals in a work of art is character—individual physiognomy', the same might be said of a judgement of taste, the difference between the two being intensive in respect of the creative faculty and extensive where the critical is concerned. Yet while one faculty might be expected to imply the other, at least potentially, it is rare to find a critic of Herbert Read's distinction who has equal claims to eminence as a poet; though it is this that gives to his artistic interpretation its peculiar authority.

Seeing, then, that he speaks as a poet, as he himself admitted on one occasion, the fact that he insists continually on the intuitive basis of the judgement must be regarded as important. 'In matters of art', he writes, 'I respect my intuitions and realise that they cannot be rationalised in any particular case.' But he goes beyond this in accepting without reserve the Vician theory that it is in primitive psychology and in the pre-logical world of the imagination that the artistic impulse must be sought. This activity, as has already been said, Vico regards as primary; since, as a form of intuitive expression it arises spontaneously and is unconnected with any save the simplest and most direct form of cognition. Similarly, from his observation of the priority of poetry over both prose and metaphysics in the history of human development, and his identification of language with poetry and poetry with imaginative expression, Vico establishes 'the autonomy of the Aesthetic world' and the irreducibility of the artistic fact.

But it is not only in his express acknowledgement of the importance of Vico's theory that Read proclaims his adherence to the principles of the 'New Science', since in his own application of its method both to the history of art and to the psychological development of the individual, he maintains throughout that ontogenetic criticism, that is, criticism involving a consideration of origins, is the only basic type.

It is doubtful, however, whether experimental analysis can ever lead to more than a partial solution of aesthetic problems; for, as he himself says, it has always been the function of art 'to stretch the mind beyond the limits of the understanding' and consequently beyond the limits of any logical explanation. It is interesting therefore to observe that while his recent studies in psychology have done much to confirm this view, they have done little to extend it, since to describe art as 'the transformation of a state of neurosis' is no appreciable advance on its definition as 'the expression through the senses of states of intuition, perception or emotion peculiar to the individual'—the 'states' in any case being 'given', while the secret of the transformation is not revealed. It is probable, therefore, that despite his understanding of mental processes and his comprehensive knowledge of the history of art, of philosophy and of the related branches of science, Read's most valuable contribution to the critical study of the modern Movements is to be found in the exercise of his own powers of intuition and in his possession of the basic awareness of the poet. Nor is this surprising when one remembers how strong an emphasis hehas always placed upon sensibility and how constantly he has reiterated the statement that it is upon sensibility that everything else depends.

In itself, and as constituting a principle of aesthetic criticism, such a view is sufficiently important, but when it is recognised as a personal conviction applicable to the whole conduct of life it is seen to be pre-eminently so. For this reason there is perhaps no more characteristic passage in the whole of his writings than that in the 'Innocent Eye' (one of the most perfect things he ever wrote) where he says 'the only real experiences in life are those lived with a virgin sensibility—so that we only hear a tone once, only see a colour once, see, hear, touch, taste and smell everything once, the first time. All life is an echo of our first sensations, and we build up our consciousness, our whole mental life, by variations and combinations of these elementary sensations.' That is his creed: so that when he says that he came gradually to perceive the analogy that exists between the order of the universe, the order of art and the order of conduct, and then goes on to define art as 'pattern informed by sensibility', he is not speaking in terms of professional detachment, but from the deepest conviction of which he is capable.

To preserve the innocent eye, to look upon everything as for the first time and so to react with an Homeric freshness of feeling is, then, Herbert Read's sufficient aim as a critic. And since, in addition, no man owes more to the memories of childhood and to the scenes of his breeding than he, it is natural that he should seek to retain a sense of values implicit in a direct response and to preserve the integrity of a personal experience whence 'that force . . . which constitutes the artist's uniqueness'—proceeds.

From passages such as the foregoing his inordinate romanticism at once becomes evident. And that he is not only avowedly, but essentially romantic is borne out in every aspect of his work and personality—in his political theory no less than in his artistic preferences. But that his taste is sufficiently catholic and his judgement sufficiently sure is borne out in his appreciations of artists as far removed in spirit as Barbara Hepworth and Henry Moore and as different in character as Paul Nash and Réne Magritte.

Criticism in respect of concrete examples however is one thing; speculation is another. For it cannot be pretended that he does even partial justice to the Classical ideal in describing it as 'a contradiction of the creative impulse', on the one hand, and as 'the intellectual counterpart of a political tyranny', on the other: particularly when he goes to the other extreme in identifying the romantic spirit with the creative spirit of life and liberation. Though that there is a clear distinction between the two and that the one *tends* towards rigidity and the other towards freedom is obvious.

Whether this view is considered as special pleading on Read's part or not, the fact remains that it is only in terms of romanticism that his achievement as a poet, as a critic and as a social theorist can be understood. But as with all theorists, his individualistic and revolutionary notions of reform are always accompanied by the idealist's assumption that the standards of an altered world would correspond to those of his own dream. Thus, for him 'the only freedom that matters is the freedom to dance', the freedom to express an individual emotion and to regain the spontaneity of an earlier age and of a less conventional mode of existence.

Under these circumstances it is natural and understandable that Read should have come to regard Surrealism, which of all forms of artistic expression is the least inhibited, as 'a reaffirmation of the Romantic principle'. But while both on psychological and political grounds Surrealism might be expected to attract him, the ultimate ground of its appeal lies in the fact that he is essentially and above all a poet and one, moreover, who feels perhaps more strongly than most the vividness of those 'memory residues' and the power of that 'emotion recollected in tranquillity' from which art, no less than poetry, takes its origin. But whereas the superreal element of poetry, which arises from its associative and reminiscent character, has always been accepted, the fact that it can be introduced into painting with equal validity is less generally recognised. Nor can Surrealism, which is merely a modern revival of earlier manifestations of the poetic spirit in art, be fully understood except in these terms, since it is upon recollection, as psychology teaches, that the subconscious for the most part depends. The difference, therefore, between poetry and painting is not so much a difference of process as a difference of aspect under which an imaginative conception can be realised, so that it might not be impossible, for instance, to capture in terms of form and colour even Cocteau's elusive image—

'All night long heaven garners its marguerites'.

A fundamental irrationality would appear, then, to be one of the most obvious characteristics of poetry, since it is not from the conscious levels of experience that poetic inspiration is derived, but rather from some depth which lies beyond the limit of an analysable state. Yet to the divine frenzy of the poet there has never been any objection. So that in so far as it represents, according to Read, 'under the aspect of poetry the process of all art', there seems to be no defensible reason why painting should be confined to the representational, instead of being left free to achieve a higher synthesis or, what Croce would describe as: 'the undifferentiated unity of the perception of the real and the simple image of the possible'. Nor is the value of the achievement of such a unity limited to the aesthetic world, if Read is right when he says that 'only an art which rises above the conscious, only a transcendent or superreal art is adequate to reconcile the contradictions of our experience', and in a self-conscious age such as the present, it is in all probability, only through the influence of an art freed from inherited prejudice that the cultivation of a sense of awareness sufficient to bring about a reintegration of life can be achieved.

Yet in spite of all that Read has done to promote an understanding of the subject, it is conceivable that Surrealism will continue to be misinterpreted for an indefinite time; partly because its ultimate possibilities are not as yet realised; partly because prejudice dies hard, since it must be admitted that its exponents have done much to justify and little to correct public misconceptions in regard to them. But if they have been guilty of much that is artistically extravagant, it can only be said that a shock of some kind was needed in order to shake the complacency of an academic world and to secure the recognition of a new scale of aesthetic values.

In an essay contributed to a series on Revolutionary Art, published in 1935, Read admitted only two Movements as having both contemporary value and formative possibilities for the future. The first was Surrealism, to which, as this examination of his views has shown, he is naturally and irresistibly drawn; the second was Abstract, or more particularly, Constructive art, towards which, in spite of his admiration for individual artists, he adopts a more critical attitude. The qualifications he imposes, however, will be considered as more or less important according to the measure of agreement he commands in his refusal to recognise the distinction usually made between fine and applied art. This distinction he has always regarded as pernicious, and rightly so, in so far as it suggests that the decorative element in design is something that is extrinsic, which can be 'applied' or not without materially affecting the character of the design itself. But in that he makes a clear distinction between humanistic art which he identifies with the ends of life, and abstract art which he identifies with the means, some equivocation would seem to be involved. At the same time, he regards the art of pure form as having the most important function of all. But it is as a social function that he conceives it, and, as such, subordinate to ends that are not primarily artistic nor concerned, except indirectly, with the spiritual aims of existence, as is made clear in *Art and Industry*[1] in a passage where he says 'So long as it is difficult to satisfy one's need for abstract art in machine-made objects—that is to say, in objects of everyday use—such art fulfils a very important function'. Yet notwithstanding the fact that he goes on to assign to painters such as Piet Mondrian, Ben Nicholson and Jean Hélion a position in society equivalent to that of pure mathematicians, it is doubtful whether they would regard themselves as more than partially compensated for the minor rôle envisaged for them in the social

[1] *Art and Industry*, first edition.

life of the future. There would appear also to be some dis-
crepancy between Read's view that uniqueness is not an aesthetic
quality that cannot be sacrificed to the requirements of the Machine
Age, and that of the Constructivists themselves who, though seeking
to re-establish the plastic arts as an integral part of the life of
the community, continue to claim for their creative achieve-
ments a unique distinction and a value that is absolute. So that
although it is undeniable that art and mechanics must have a
reciprocal effect upon one another in an age such as the present, the
question as to whether or not 'a standardized object' can possess
'intuitional form' in a degree equal to that of a work independently
conceived is as debatable as the statement that 'the true kind of
artist, the only kind of artist we need, apart from the humanistic
artist (that is, the painter of landscapes and portraits, etc.) is merely
the workman with the best aptitude for design'. Yet despite Read's
insistence on this point, it is difficult to accept it as final, since (with
a charming and characteristic inconsistency, for which he would be
the last to apologize) he maintains elsewhere that 'art begins where
function ends', being as it is 'essentially disinterested'.

Generally speaking, Read's theory of education may be said to be
based on a frank acceptance of the principles of the Bauhaus school,
to which he is attracted by a natural predisposition. The aims of this
school, which was founded by Dr. Gropius at Weimar in 1919, but has
since been established in America, may be briefly summarized as
follows: the first is to keep alive the child's sincerity of emotion,
fantasy and creativeness; the second to strive towards the timeless
elements of biological expression; and the third to take as the
basis of education the development of man as an organic whole. In
other words, the aim of the school is to train and to develop the
sensibilities to the fullest possible extent, to which end the most
advanced technical and scientific methods are used, but the
object of the workshops, in which the organization centres, is to
produce the craftsman and not the artist, who must always and
in any case remain an exception. It is, thus, in accordance with
the principles of the Bauhaus that Read sets forth his argument
in favour of the development of education on a technical basis;
of the abolition of the art schools (and justifiably so, since they
can seldom lead to the production of more than an average competence, and artistic mediocrity serves only to confuse the issue)
and to the re-establishment of some system of apprenticeship, in

order 'to reunite what should never have been separated', in the words of Eric Gill, namely, 'the man as artist and the man as craftsman'—in which sense Read is warranted in regarding the popular distinction made between the artist and the ordinary man as invidious.

The material advantages belonging to an educational system of this kind are, however, of less importance than the ethical principle it involves. Also because education is, in its very nature, a concern of the individual and 'the cultivation of the individual the root of everything else' the importance of introducing a more enlightened, a more thorough and a more honest system cannot be over-estimated. It is encouraging, too, to think that its adumbration in an age that is characterised by superficiality on the one hand and pretentiousness on the other, and in which in fact 'plain living and high thinking are no more' (though the one if not the other is rapidly being forced upon us) may indicate the coming of a new and more vigorous order, or of what Vico would describe as a 'reflux' in the cyclic periods of history. But while opinions must necessarily differ as to the best means of securing the ends desired, of the need for a revaluation of the standards of life and conduct, on which point Read continually insists, there can be no doubt.

In this process the artist as a social being has a vital and formative part to play, though, as an expression of the highest potentialities of the age, he is not generated by historical conditions, but is himself, as Read has pointed out, 'the precedent fact'. He has therefore a social function to perform that is neither inferior to that of the scientist, nor intrinsically different from that of the philosopher or the divine. But because the *uses* of art are intensive and belong, like those of music and mathematics, to the moral ends of life in a Socratic sense not on that account are the interests of society any the less well served. That is to say, it is only to the extent to which art is removed from all political influence and to which it is left free to develop in accordance with the laws of its own nature that its integrity as a cultural influence can be preserved. It can never, therefore, be organised nor made to fit the requirements of a particular social pattern, no matter how excellent such a pattern may seem to be. On the contrary, it might even be said that the virtue of any form of society is in the degree of its approximation to the absolute standards of the aesthetic world. But inasmuch as the attainment of such a standard is synonymous with culture, and culture, as Read has shown, represents 'a slow product of the organic process we call history', it follows inevitably that it cannot be imposed either by legislation or by the bureaucratic methods which he abhors. For notwithstanding his instinct for social reform and his perception of its need, he is, in the last analysis, primarily concerned with the individual, whom, in contradistinction to the state, he has designated as the 'only reality'. Yet in his anxiety to promote the desired changes, he has perhaps overlooked the fact that he himself already possesses powers more potent than any others to effect them, powers which Shelley (a poet to whom he bears in some ways a curious resemblance) signalised in his *Defence of Poetry* when he said that 'the great instrument of moral good is the imagination' and that 'poets are the unacknowledged legislators of the world'.

The conclusion is thus inescapable that political systems are, by comparison, unimportant, though this is not to say that much might not be accomplished by enlightened reforms. As Read remarks, however, 'sincerity is not truth; it is only conviction'; while the time is not yet come when philosophers may be kings.

Yet it is perhaps after all as well that this should be so, when one considers the fundamental impracticability of the idealist's notions, which are invariably based, as has been said, on the assumption that his own stage of development represents the norm; whereas, of course, nothing could be further from the truth. Nor in this respect is Read an exception to the rule, as witness his professed belief in anarchy and more particularly what he understands by it. For him anarchy means the complete absence of rule to the end that man may be free to pursue the Taoist way of reflection and to live his life in accordance with its principles. But as this requires the moral control of an ascetic and the spiritual concentration of a sage it hardly seems suited to a society that is lacking, for the most part, in even the rudiments of culture and in those qualities which he rightly regards as elementary, namely, gentleness, grace and reverence in its manners and in its speech.

No single aspect of Read's work can be fully understood or appreciated, however, without reference to the others which are regressively implied. Thus his conception of art and of its place in society leads naturally to the consideration of political forms, the consideration of political forms to the contemplation of human destiny, the contemplation of human destiny to the dreams of the poet, and the dreams of the poet to the deepest characteristics of the man himself.

'My profoundest experiences', he writes in the *Annals of Innocence and Experience*, 'have been not religious nor moral, but aesthetic'—a statement which provides the measure of all the rest. But aesthetic experience is not *necessarily* pleasurable, except by an elliptical usage of the word, and in his own case, at least, the nostalgic element, and even a deeper consciousness of pain is implicit, as may be seen in the direct expression of his feeling as a poet. Yet even so he is less preoccupied with the remembrance of personal suffering than filled with a spirit of bitterness and with a profound pity for human wrong and for the agonies of—

'A world too strong in folly for the bliss of dreams.'

And that this is expressive of an intense and spontaneous emotion is borne out not only by the fact that he has always sought as far as possible to avoid the imposition of any conscious control on his forms (an aim which proves his affinity with the Surrealists), but also by the internal evidence of the poems themselves, which represent for him the expression of something fundamental to his being and something in respect of which he has no choice.

Everything thus contributes to prove that insight, sensibility and compassion are the qualities by which he is pre-eminently distinguished. And if in the whole of English poetry there are any lines which might be said to epitomise his attitude as a critic, as a poet and as a man, there are none that have more peculiar relevance than those in Shelley's 'Hymn to Intellectual Beauty':

> '. . . that never joy illumed my brow
> Unlinked with hope that thou wouldst free
> This world from its dark slavery.'

That is enough: for therein lies the complete justification of his creed that 'the highest manifestation of the immanent will of the universe is the work of art'.

H. W. HÄUSERMANN

THE DEVELOPMENT OF HERBERT READ[1]

1. Origins and Characteristics

An ideal of beauty that finds its most appropriate expression in reflective lyrics, or even in didactic poetry, has always formed part of the English conception of art. The work of Herbert Read follows this more than any other tendency in the English tradition. Though his poetry cannot be called didactic in the proper sense of the word, ideas are the main source of his inspiration. The clue to his critical and aesthetic work lies in the fact that he believes this kind of poetry to represent art in its highest form. On the other hand his writings, mainly those after 1931, reflect a different attitude: appreciation for unreflective art, for an art that entirely abandons the realm of conscious reason. With a glance cautious but full of expectation he bends over to gaze at the mysterious and creative depth of the human soul. And in so doing Herbert Read does justice to that other side of his nature which seeks fulfilment not in the universality of thought but in the spontaneity of feeling.

Herbert Read, a Yorkshire farmer's son, who for three years fought at the front in the last war, shows all the tenacity and indestructible toughness of his race. Where, through the experience of war, many youths of his age were driven to despair of this world, he emerged with his sense of reality unimpaired. His memories of war lack any false sentimentality. In 1926 Richard Aldington, a critic as competent on this subject as one could wish for, called Read's war book *In Retreat*: 'the only English book I have seen (i.e. on the war) which does succeed in communicating a section of real experience'[2]). Across a greater distance of time, H. G. Porteus comes to the conclusion: '(Read) is in any case the greatest of the war poets'.[3] Only someone who like Read has preserved so pure a relation to the instinctive foundations of life could have described

[1] *Studien zur Englischen Literarkritik, 1910–1930*, Publ. by Heinrich Poeppinghaus O.H.-G. 1938, Bochum Langendreer.

[2] *New Criterion*, April 1926, p. 364.   [3] *Criterion*, April 1935, p. 706.

the horrors of the battlefield with the objectivity of *In Retreat* and *The End of a War*.

Read's early contacts with peasants and craftsmen have given his mind a direction that made him a literary critic of quite a special brand. His preference for what is plastic, concrete and of good craftsmanship has supplied his art theories with a certain solid robustness, which is perhaps not quite compatible with literary refinement. Read has always been more artist than art critic. This perhaps explains why he was not recognised as one of the best English critics till 1930. In that little masterpiece *The Innocent Eye* (1933) where Read describes his childhood spent on his father's farm, one finds the sentence: 'The perturbations of the intellect are a danger to the instinctive basis of life; no wonder, then, that nature is wise enough to wrap us in a cocoon of insensibility, until such time as we have the power to counter intelligence with deeper intuitions.'[1] Read has never failed to listen to these deeper intuitions; on the other hand he has also been led on by a merely discursive intelligence. For any critical examination of his work it is necessary to distinguish these two sources of perception.

Even a consideration of Read's literary methods gives one an idea of an artistic nature in which feeling plays an important part. He does not write like a scholar who builds up his work methodically and with regularity. With every new book he makes a new start. Every new book, however planned it may appear in its structure, betrays the poet impatient to communicate, the poet whom a sudden leap carries away from and beyond logical concepts. His formulation is such that it does not admit of any contradiction. His inner vision draws to itself everything that can be of use to it, silencing any critical objections. Read's thought is aphoristic, and therefore particularly suited for the essay. Where he attempts to create more systematically and on a larger scale he is not so successful.

His keen and vital intellect is matched by an open-eyed unbiased judgment. His two main subjects—literary criticism and the history of art—open for him the way to all other spheres of culture. He is widely read and shows critical understanding in every field. There may be other critics of his time his superiors in scientific training or in verbal magic: there are not many that are his equals in universality of interest and richness of aesthetic feeling.

The other pole of Read's personality, his sense of order, his deep respect for the laws of nature, is best explained by his peasant

[1] Page 70.

descent. It is this peculiar quality of mind which from an early date has secured him his particular rôle in English literary criticism of the twenties.[1] By his essays on *Reason and Romanticism* (1926) he has taken sides with the new generation whose representatives— in opposition to the sceptics of the post-war period—assume an affirmative attitude towards life. Now the moral problem in its widest sense is put into the centre. While hitherto only aesthetic, psychological or sociological questions had been dealt with, and in a purely theoretical fashion, it is now the demand for value, for a compelling notion of Good that enters into the foreground of aesthetic research. As early as in the middle 'thirties the new moralists divide themselves into two distinctly different tendencies. One—the innerworldly one—is represented by Middleton Murry, and in France by R. Fernandez. The other tendency is represented by T. S. Eliot, Read and the American neo-humanists. The first tendency seeks and finds its highest value in a heightened humanity, in a strict discipline of soul, comparable to the physical training of the athlete. The other tendency sets its criterion outside man, either in a manifest religion or in another sphere of values, which can only be established by constant search.

For Read this highest norm has always been Reason. His early essays —though on widely different subjects—all pursue this one aim: to link into a greater unity under the sign of 'reason' all the manifold manifestations of art: classic and romantic, lyricism of thought and of feeling, comedy and tragedy, fancy and imagination. Even to-day Read's thought moves around this centre. As late as 1936 he points to his definition formulated for the first time ten years earlier: '(Reason) is often used as a synonym for rationality, or even for a mechanistic logic. Reason should rather connote the widest evidence of the senses, and of all processes and instincts developed in the long history of man. It is the sum total of awareness, ordained and ordered to some specific end or object of attention.'[2] The more simply, the more concretely this conception of Reason is understood, the more it corresponds to Read's sense of order, to the ingrained conviction of the peasant and pre-critical man, that 'the evidence of the senses' represents the ultimate measure of everything existing. Expressed in metaphysical terms Read's Reason has its philosophical analogy most clearly in the Universals of Thomism. In art it forms the base of all aesthetic enjoyment: 'Art thus only gives joy

[1] Cf. T. S. Eliot's review of Read's first volume of essays in *The New Criterion*, Oct. 1926, pp. 751 f.

[2] *Reason and Romanticism*, p. 27; cf. also *Surrealism*, pp. 22 f., footnote.

in proportion to the understanding we bring to it, and our understanding must be of the most universal and sympathetic kind.'[1]

2. *The Profession of the Critic*

The concept of poetic mission, which Paul Meissner applied to English literary criticism in general and which insists on the close relation of poetry to life,[2] is also the cardinal point of Read's programme as traced in his essay *The Attributes of Criticism*.[3] Characteristic of Read's special purpose, as also of the development of all English criticism since 1900, is that he should oppose two tendencies in vogue during this period. The first is that hedonist impressionistic form of criticism that likes to avoid taking up an attitude towards anything new and experimental by regarding art in the easy and traditional way, as something merely to be enjoyed. Read does not mention names, but he has in mind Edmund Gosse, Walter Raleigh, Clutton-Brook, J. C. Squire, Edward Shanks, Robert Lynd and John Freeman. Read's negative judgment on these critics hits the point: 'To appreciate the flexible tendency of one's mind—to float with the current of one's likes and dislikes (and that is legitimate enough when the current flows steadily in one direction)—by such means a tolerable body of criticism may be evolved. But there comes a time when it is possible to see the vanity of one's own gesticulations, and then conscience cries Stop. Your particular opinions, given upon every or several occasions, tend to immerse you in their particularity.'[4] Read reproaches these critics with their incapacity to grasp the ethical value implicit in art as in anything else; he accuses them of solipsism, and points to the teachings of St. Thomas as the only salvation from that egocentricity by which they are threatened.

On the other hand Read is as firm in opposing the pragmatic form of literary judgment, represented in his opinion by I. A. Richards. The highest ethical values for him being objects of intuition, he cannot tolerate that the value of a work of art should be made subject to its utility. Nowhere does Read's fundamentally ethical conception of art—in the sense of the above-mentioned essay by Paul Meissner—show itself more impressively than in his discussion of the *Principles of Literary Criticism* of which he says

[1] *Reason and Romanticism*, p. 26.

[2] Deutsche Vierteljahrsschrift, Issue I, 1936. *The Idea of Poetic Mission in English Literary Criticism.*

[3] *Reason and Romanticism*, pp. 1–29. [4] Ibid., p. 3.

in conclusion: '(Richards) assumes, rather arbitrarily, that ethics is necessarily a matter of "such crude valuations as may be codified in a moral". But what if the difficulty of associating moral values with art is a question, not so much of a wrong conception of art, but rather a wrong conception of ethics. Mr. Richards despairs of ethics without examining the possibilities of a reconstruction of that science as vital as the one he would effect in literary criticism. . . . Mr. Richards would avoid the difficulty by a frank acceptance of utilitarian or prudential ethics. The fact that Mr. Richards ignores, or denies, is the existence of a moral consciousness. . . . Art demands a sanction, as every other activity.'[1] He concedes to Richards' doctrine only one positive quality: that it breaks with that aestheticism and ethically indifferent impressionism, which in its turn is to be understood as a reaction against the school led by Ruskin and Arnold.

Read has later on expressed his opinion about two other forms of criticism: favourably towards the introspective line taken by R. Fernandez, unfavourably towards T. S. Eliot's dogmatic attitude to art. In Fernandez he finds philosophical serenity—such a rare gift in a critic, and one that Goethe possessed to an extraordinarily high degree. 'It is not ridiculous to confront Mr. Fernandez and Goethe: both have the same concern for the development of the personality, for the perfection of character, and they both look at literature from this point of view.'[2]

Read's ethical conception of the development of personality, however, has nothing to do with puritanical zeal and severity. Since his conversion to the anglican faith Eliot, in Read's opinion, has committed a mistake which to-day is unpardonable: he has fallen back into the 'moralistic confusion' of a Ruskin and an Arnold. He is even accused of hypocritical distortion by condemning Shelley's morals, by opposing his ideas to the neglect of his poetry.[3]

However fiercely Read turns against a dogmatic, especially puritanical order of values, he firmly sticks to his conviction that there are norms, ethical norms to which even art is subjected. Read compares the critic to a man 'who has carefully elaborated a few dogmas, in the sure belief that without such fixed points no course can be steered, no height measured, and no distances maintained. But having fixed his points, he does not stand still; he is impelled in some direction, and the force that drives him is feeling or emotion.

[1] *The Criterion*, April 1925, pp. 448 f.
[2] *The New Adelphi*, December 1927, p. 171.
[3] *In Defence of Shelley*, 1936.

That is the final test of criticism: that its methods are perfected in science, but that the motives are spontaneous, impulsive—aspects of courage, constancy and devotion.'[1] This metaphorical definition does not imply much more than a resolve and a confession. Everything depends as before on the good will, for a clear definition of the aim of critical effort is still lacking. The tone of his pronouncements is determined enough: 'A significant mind is only significant by virtue of its organisation and the intellect is the only organising faculty known to man. It is the only ultimate measure of values, and values are the only end of criticism.'[2] What is missing is a clear philosophical conception. 'Although the post-war period is only ten years old we are still unable to state our characteristic beliefs. Our fathers had some sort of faith, materialistic or religious, but to-day all who think are still full of doubt.'[3]

What part does Read assign to science? How can psychology help the critic who considers it his main task to judge art in accordance with the highest values of reason? By accepting this as his main task the critic runs the risk of losing contact with the natural foundations of a work of art, of becoming absorbed in sophisticated aesthetic distinctions. To psychology, therefore, he must constantly turn for the empirical confirmation of his intuitive discoveries. In this sense psychology becomes for the critic an auxiliary science, whose methods he need not always use, but whose results are always relevant.

3. Read's pre-psycho-analytical theory of art

Read seems to have become acquainted with psycho-analysis at a comparatively late stage. His essay on 'The Nature of Metaphysical Poetry'[4] published as late as 1923 shows no trace of Freud's teachings. This essay pursues a double aim. It firstly seeks to answer historical queries about the precursors of the English metaphysical poets. 'The philosophical spirit in both Donne and Chapman was, I think, derived directly from Dante and the early Italian poets, rather than from more immediate forerunners in Spain and France.'[5] Secondly—here of greater importance—Read undertakes the task of finding a psychological explanation for this peculiar metaphysical lyric. This explanation, though still based on the

---

[1] *Reason and Romanticism*, p. 44.
[2] *The New Criterion*, June 1926, p. 611.
[3] *The Criterion*, Dec. 1938, 'Humanism and the Absolute', p. 270.
[4] *The Criterion*, April 1923, p. 246. [5] *Reason and Romanticism*, p. 44.

venerable faculty type of psychology, points already, in its distinct emphasis on feeling, to the subsequent turn to psycho-analysis.

Even before 1923 T. S. Eliot and Aldous Huxley had described metaphysical poetry as 'sensuous apprehension of thought' or as 'felt thought'. Thus Read says nothing new in repeating 'I will define it as the emotional apprehension of thought'.[1] He is only original in the dogged determination with which he heads for a psycho-physical explanation. The link 'from under', with the biologic-physiological regions, must be established at any cost. This can be done only by isolating the emotional content of the metaphysical lyric. 'It is necessary at all costs to maintain a nexus between lyrical poetry and metaphysical poetry in the word "poetry"; and since I despise all distinctions based on the technique or décor of poetry, I prefer to justify this nexus in the word *emotion*, which denotes a common foundation in physical fact.'[2] He goes even further: an exact description of all literary phenomena, he maintains, should start from the fact that certain glandular secretions are correlated to definite sensations and feelings.[3] Even in his more mature works Read has preserved his readiness to accept a vitalistic (not a mechanistic) biology. A passage typical of this attitude we find in his *English Prose Style* (1928): 'The voice has its visceral controls, and though it would be rash to assume that the rhythmical reactions of the viscera and larynx to a strong emotion *are* the rhythms of the accompanying speech, yet these physical connections should be remembered since they are the basis of those refinements of expression which art introduces. What else is art, or conscience and intelligence for that matter, but a subtle extenuation and spiritualisation of the gross physical responses of the body to its environment?'[4]

While in I. A. Richards we trace the influence of the scientific and mathematical thought of Cambridge, Read reflects rather more the spirit of Oxford. Here William McDougall used to be Reader in Mental Philosophy, and fundamentally Read has never left the philosophical ground of McDougall's doctrine. McDougall deliberately opposes the old English tradition of psychology that, starting with Locke, reaches over Hume and the Associationists to Watson's behaviourism. McDougall adheres to the same 'dionysian' or hormic conception of the soul which is to-day represented by Bergson, Freud, the Gestalt School, and similar theories. 'Modern psychology', says McDougall, 'the psycho-analytic speciality no less

[1] *Reason and Romanticism*, p. 35.   [2] Ibid., pp. 34 f.   [3] Ibid., p. 33.
[4] Loc. cit., pp. 165 f.

than the more academic and comprehensive hormic psychology, is showing that the indispensable term *instinct*, or instinctive endowment, points to something far more subtle and profoundly influential than a congenital mechanical reflex or any bundle of such reflexes.'[1] Read forms his fundamental conception of reason quite in keeping with McDougall. As Rudolf Metz points out in his characterisation of the English psychologist, reason is understood not so much as a self-existing phenomenon, but rather as rising from the instinctive categories.[2]

This philosophical attitude is the essential thing. As compared to that, it is not very significant that Read cannot use McDougall's teachings about the instincts and their relations to the emotions for his immediate purpose: to explain the psychology of the metaphysical poets. After having linked poetry to a physical basis by way of feeling, he continues: 'The business of the literary critic is to identify the mental rather than the physiological significance of the material in his hands, and in this sense a more useful distinction can be made in the content of the emotions;'[3] whereupon he divides the emotions into those with abstract and those with concrete content.

The emotion evoked by a simple lyrical poem has a concrete content, that caused by a didactic poem an abstract one. The complete inadequacy of this explanation, which in disregarding the unique creative act wants to put in its place a kind of functional formalism, is revealed by the following space- and timebound mechanical metaphor: 'As an illustration we might represent thought and emotion as two separately revolving pulleys: One, emotion, has a revolution a thousand times greater than the other; but by the operation of a lever the two pulleys are connected, and immediately thought is accelerated to the speed or intensity of emotion.'[4]

4. *The Advent of Psycho-analysis*

In the January 1925 issue of the *Criterion* appears Read's essay on 'Psycho-analysis and the Critic' which later, enlarged and under the title 'Psycho-Analysis and Criticism', is incorporated in the collected volume *Reason and Romanticism*. This essay shows for the first time Read's attitude towards the new psychology, his views

[1] *The Frontiers of Psychology* (1934), pp. 186 f.
[2] *Die philosophischen Stroemungen der Gegenwart in Grossbritannien* (1935), vol. ii, p. 301.
[3] *Reason and Romanticism*, p. 34.   [4] Ibid., p. 38.

on the usefulness of the psycho-analytical categories for literary criticism, and his particular way of interpreting these categories from an aesthetic point of view. In a wider sense this essay is also historically significant for literary criticism in general. For in this essay Read, no longer satisfied with the old tradition of emotional criticism, makes himself the speaker for a new movement, which, relating itself to Coleridge, aims at a more serious philosophical and aesthetic attitude.[1]

Let Read speak for himself first. It would be surprising if he agreed with the views previously held by scholars like Ernest Jones, F. C. Prescott, Joseph Collins and Albert Mordell.[2] It is against his artistic nature to look at poetry only through the eyes of a doctor. He also realises that psycho-analysis and kindred doctrines are still far from satisfying the claims of strict science and philosophy.[3] Read likes to see himself as the man of letters who ventures into the field of psycho-analysis merely as an amateur, adopting from it whatever meets the occasion. He talks of himself as 'a mere expropriator in this territory'[4] supplementing the scientific results by introspection, unconcerned whether this procedure is against the rules. He is convinced that the critic can arrive at the right judgment merely by applying universal principles, 'but psycho-analysis might be a shorter path to the test; and in any case it would supply collateral evidence of a very satisfactory kind.'[5] And for psychology there also remains the task of reducing those universal principles to their special categories.

Read's conversion to psycho-analysis is but one aspect of that greater revolution in English literary criticism that takes place in the post-war years, and whereby for the school of Gosse and Raleigh is substituted a literary criticism with a higher philosophical standard. Seen from this angle psycho-analysis is the continuation of Herbert Spencer's physio-philosophical criticism. Art criticism that had become divorced from nature is led back to it by science. 'There is no need to make a mystery of art', Read declares, basing himself on that 'general law of determinism to which all our emotions and ideals are bound.'[2] This is the key note for most of the literary criticism of the nineteen-twenties.

---

[1] Cf. T. S. Eliot, 'Experiment in Criticism', *Tradition and Experiment*, Oxford University Press, 1929.

[2] Cf. L. Cazamian, *Criticism in the Making*, 1929, pp. 86 f.

[3] Cf. Roland Dalbiez, *La méthode psychanalytique et la doctrine freudienne*, 1937.

[4] *Reason and Romanticism*, p. 88.   [5] Ibid., p. 99.

All the time Read remains conscious of the fact that his real task, that of discerning values in art, differs fundamentally from that of the merely explaining psychologist. For the latter, the importance of a work of art lies in its symptomatic character; it allows him to explore the workings of the unconscious on the lines of the genetic principle. He is interested in the subject matter and the motives, not in the beauty of the work of art; while Read makes a clear distinction between the symbol and the symptom. 'Analysis involves the reduction of the symbol to its origins, and once the symbol is in this way dissolved it is of no aesthetic significance: art is art as symbol, not as sign,'[1] and even more emphatically: 'Any explanation that psychology can offer for the complicated strands of poetic creation tends to quicken our general sensibility. Reasoning and mechanism do not lose their value because we follow step by step the process of their operation; and I think a poetic process is exactly analogous. It is where you have, not a dynamic process, but a static symbol, that analysis is without any critical significance, and may be positively destructive of the aesthetic effect.'[2] The poetic process is not a mystery; it is open to the analytical mode of perception of the psychologist; but however profound the psychological associations a poem offers to a penetrating analysis, its artistic value can only be assessed by the critic. The influence of psychology on literary criticism has not been so thorough as to destroy the respect for creative genius. The analyst can only bring the work of art closer to the critic. The critic's final judgment, however, springs from intuition, and is not ultimately determined by insight into the creative process however profound an insight it may be.

The interpretation of poetic imagination forms the centre of Read's researches into the psychology of literature. For the professional psychologist too this problem is the basis of research, the clue to all the other aspects of creative personality.[3] The problem of poetic imagination is the most frequent point of contact between literary criticism and the tendencies derived from psychology. Read makes use of this mutual clarification in two directions. In the first place, by going into the mechanism of the unconscious, the general aspect of all creative activity. On this interpretation will depend how to explain those literary conceptions which gain in lucidity from psychological analysis: classic and romantic, the myth, the metaphor, fancy and imagination, humour and wit. By the

---

[1] *Reason and Romanticism*, p. 86.   [2] Ibid., p. 87, footnote.
[3] Cf. Walter Muschg, *Psychoanalyse und Lit. Wiss.*, 1930.

same means more light is also shed on problematic and much disputed poetic personalities like Shelley, the sisters Brontë, Jane Austen. His next preoccupation is with the solution of the problem of value, which Read attempted once before through psychology. It was however his only attempt, though official science does not at all exclude the possibility of such a solution. Writing on the stronger psychological element in modern aesthetics, C. K. Ogden states in the *Encyclopaedia Britannica* (1926): 'An important influence leading in the same direction has been that of psycho-analysis with its fresh light on the growth and development of preferences. Though at present easily misapplied in criticism, its consequences, especially for the study of creative imagination, are likely to be fundamental.'[1] Since 1935 Read has never repeated this attempt, seeing more and more clearly that the approach to a doctrine of values must be found from the side of philosophy, and not through the roundabout way of psychology. It is also possible that I. A. Richards' failure in this field has come to him as a warning.

5. The Years 1925 to 1930

The years 1930–31 bring about a fundamental change in Read's spiritual attitude. Also his views on the essence of art and of creative imagination acquire some important limitations. We are therefore justified in first examining separately the psychological explanations of poetry he offered in the second half of the 'twenties.

The peculiarity of Read's thought during this period lies in his assigning a predominant part to reason in every field. For instance, he rejects the orthodox conception expressed in Ernest Jones's *Essays in Applied Psycho-Analysis* (1923): the belief that the artist's yearning for ideal beauty can be understood ontogenetically from the child's reaction to his excremental interests. The repression of those instincts may, in Read's view, play a part; it is however not sufficient 'to account for the variety and profundity of aesthetic expression in general.'[2] He suggests that a more adequate theory of motivation is to be found in Alfred Adler. It is the experiences of adolescence which more than anything else cause inferiority complexes, experiences which lead to sharp conflicts between instinctive egotistic desires and social taboos. 'I think there can be

---

[1] Vol. 29, p. 45.
[2] *Reason and Romanticism*, p. 96.

no doubt that the artist is born of this conflict.'[1] The artist resembles the neurotic in that he escapes from this conflict into an imaginary world of his desire. While the neurotic, however, is not capable of clothing the creations of his imagination with formal beauty, the artist can escape the danger of his disposition and make his way back into reality. The wish to become like God, which by the ordinary healthy person is repressed into the Unconscious, is taken seriously by the artist, and becomes for him the motive of his will to form. He masters his neurosis thanks to his 'ideal or affective tendency', by which Read understands a forceful inclination for order, form and harmony. This universal element reflecting reason, the antidote of the emotional and haphazard, contains in Read's opinion the true essence of art. Read provides numerous evidences of this rational ideal of art. I quote the two perhaps most conclusive ones: 'Emotions in subjection—that is the very definition of Art!', and at greater length in that confessional essay 'The Nature of Poetry': 'Science and poetry have but one ideal, which is the satisfaction of the reason . . . in symmetry, in rhythm, and in all the properties of universal truth.'[2]

The fullest description of the creative process, as Read sees it, is found in the essay on 'Psycho-analysis and Criticism': 'What really happens may perhaps be described in the following way: you have in the first place the prevailing affectivity, the latent ideal of form or thought. . . . You have, next, the bringing into activity fortuitously of some image or memory, which until the moment of inspiration had lain latent in the unconscious mind; this fortuitous image is as it were criticised by the excited interest; it is selected or rejected; and if selected it is developed and transformed by the ever prevalent affectivity. If the affective tendency is suddenly and strongly roused, then you get a state of emotion, bringing with it an intensity of awareness to all the images and ideas that follow in the wake of the first fortuitous image. This is the state of ecstasy. Images seem to leap from their hiding-places all fully equipped for the service of the ideal or affective tendency.'[3] Other descriptions of the same process are to be found frequently within the next five years.[4] Apart from irrelevant deviations they all show the same characteristics: the substance of the work of art has its roots in the unconscious, while form springs from an ideal, which though operating unconsciously is wholly within the sphere of reason,

[1] *Reason and Romanticism*, p. 97.   [2] Ibid., p. 58.   [3] Ibid., pp. 94 f.
[4] Cf. *English Prose Style* (1928), pp. 165 f., *Phases of English Poetry* (1928), pp. 78 f., *Wordsworth* (1930), pp. 160 f.

dominating over the whole of consciousness. These two opposites, the unconscious and the ideal of order, balance each other in the finished work of art: 'I think that in the mind of every artist (though I think particularly of the literary artist) there are two contrary tendencies. In one direction he is impelled to shuffle off conscious control and to sink back into his primitive mind, where he knows he can find a fresh elemental imagery, a rich though incoherent phantasy. It is the disjointed fortuitous world of dreams—day-dreams. In the other direction he is impelled to establish strong affective tendencies—ideals of moral beauty, of plastic form, of order and architecture. . . . You get the harmony of perfect art when the two forces achieve a balance.'[1] On this basis Read explains romantic and classical art by the predominance of one or the other of these forces.

For the analysis of the creative artistic process Read has availed himself mainly of conceptions taken from individual psychology. We must, however, also mention a definition which he derives from the doctrine of C. G. Jung. Read quotes a passage from the English edition of *Psychological Types*, which runs as follows: 'Active phantasy being the principal attribute of the artistic mentality, the artist is not merely a *representer*: he is also a *creator*, hence essentially an educator, since his works have the value of symbols that trace out the line of the future development.'

'Whether the actual social validity of the symbol is more general or more restricted depends on the quality or vital capacity of the creative individuality. The more abnormal the individual, i.e. the less his general fitness for life, the more limited will be the common social value of the symbols he produces, although their value may be absolute for the individuality in question.'[2]

Read bases all his hope on this 'actual social validity', He believes to have discovered in it nothing less than an objective standard of value for aesthetic criticism. Starting from the assumption, 'that the poetic function is nothing but this active phantasy in its more-than-individual aspect',[3] he registers an important conformity between the psychological and the critical mode of work. He believes that the social validity of the symbol and so the artistic value of a poem can be established by subjecting it to an analysis by means of Freud's reductive method. 'Psycho-analysis finds in art a system of symbols, representing a hidden reality, and by analysis it can testify to the purposive genuineness of the symbols;

[1] *Reason and Romanticism,* pp. 92 f.
[2] Loc. cit., pp. 655 f.   [3] *Reason and Romanticism,* pp. 90 f.

it can also testify to the faithfulness, the richness and the range of the mind behind the symbol.'[1] Here is a possibility of establishing values which Read has however not pursued any further, though it is one which had been thought particularly promising.[2]

Read misunderstands the meaning of Freud's method if he expects from it something more than the mere practical result of an elimination of conflicts. On the other hand he is inclined, with Jung, to see in art the expression of the collective unconscious. He sets great faith in the possibility 'of relating the types actualised by the poetic imagination to their origin in the root-images of the community. In this way criticism would possess still another basic reality on which it could ground the imaginative hypotheses of art.'[3] But how to carry out this synthetical interpretation in practice, remains an unsolved problem for him, a problem for which Jung himself, as it happens, does not know a satisfactory solution.[4] What attracts Read more than anything else in Jung's hypothesis, is the conception of a super-individual, ideal sphere in which reside those 'collective images called ideals'[5] that form the essence of art. Unlike Jung Read always presupposes a conflict between the ideal and the emotion, a struggle between order and chaos from which, as a third element, art is born. The emotion becomes subdued, instinct tamed. Though for Jung the archetypes appear in the formed subject-matter as regulative principles of its forming, their presence calls rather for a freeing of emotion. Jung describes the same process quite differently from Read: 'The moment which initiates a mythological situation is always characterised by a special emotional intensity; it feels like striking chords in us that have never sounded before, or as if forces had been freed of whose existence we never had any idea.'[6]

The contradictions in Read's theory of the poetic imagination are numerous; they are easily discovered even by a person untrained in psychology. Not only are the invoked authorities with their different presuppositions used without distinction in support of Read's theory, without their field of application having been duly

---

[1] *Reason and Romanticism*, p. 99.

[2] Cf. A. W. Ramsay, 'Psychology and Literary Criticism', *The Criterion*, July 36, pp. 631 f.

[3] Loc. cit., pp. 106.

[4] *Seelenprobleme der Gegenwart*, 2nd ed., 1932, pp. 112 f.

[5] Ibid., p. 70.

[6] Ibid., 'Ueber die Beziehungen der analytischen Psychologie zum dichterischen Kunstwerk', pp. 69 f. This essay was first published in *Wissen und Leben*, May 1922. It may not have been known to Read.

defined—but within this conception itself too there are incongruities of a major character. At the root of all his errors is perhaps his dualistic philosophy of faculties, as he applied it in his essay on metaphysical poetry. This dualism was never abandoned in spite of the introduction of a few psycho-analytical conceptions and expressions. Reason has merely been replaced by the affective tendencies, emotion by the unconscious. Neither Jung nor Adler know of a fundamental antagonism between the unconscious and the conscious, or for that matter between instinct and intellect. Both regions, for Adler, have their place in the striving for perfection of personality; while for Jung they are subjected to the influence of a binding power centred in the collective sphere. For Read however the contrast between the two regions means everything; the father of art is conflict.

Spontaneous emotion therefore seems to him the great foe to be overcome by the arms of the spirit. But at the same time this emotion represents for him the inexhaustible source from which poetry gains its strength. For, in spite of his classicist doctrine Read is essentially a romantic. In early Italian poetry, as in Donne and Chapman, he admires most of all their lyrical power by which even the most uncongenial, unpoetic ideas are dissolved in emotion. In Dante all experience, that of the senses and the imagination as well as that of reason, is transformed into song. Even in a late poet like Wordsworth metaphysical poetry is the expression of his whole personality. The poetry of to-day, in Read's view, is marked by the incapacity of bringing thought and emotion to an artistic balance.[1] It may be that this opinion reflects only his own incapacity as projected into the period. While for I. A. Richards 'synaesthetics' covers not only the psychological phenomena of art, but—in its biological effect—also its value, Read assigns to art cognitive value. For him too, as has been shown, a certain balance of impulses is of decisive importance; all the same he does not see in art merely 'an extraordinarily successful device' in the service of the organism.[2] Art has not just got a therapeutical function in the psycho-analytical meaning of successful sublimation and solution of conflict. Poetry to Read means the emotional apprehension of thought and thus of reality. The more reason is embodied in a poem the greater its value. Of course reason, in this connection, must not be taken for discursive ratio but for intuitive introspection. One can see how closely Read has approached the conception of Croce.

[1] *Reason and Romanticism*, pp. 46 f.   [2] *Practical Criticism*, p. 277.

6. Transformation

At this stage it is not possible to understand to the full the change which since 1930 Read has undergone in his ideas on art. All the same one can already point out some of the causes that have led to his new attitude. It is also quite possible to underline a few characteristics, we think important, of the process of transformation which he is at present passing through, and to explain these characteristics in the light of the period.

First the impact of the political situation.

After the failure of the General Strike in 1926 England's economical situation had worsened at an alarming rate. Only by the drastic measures taken by the National Government between 1931 and 1935 did the country slowly recover from the state of distress into which it had been thrown by the crisis in world-economy. But this state of distress had its after-effects. A great many of the English intellectuals are today prepared to subscribe to socialism of a British brand. This English form of communism differs in essential points from the continental and more Marxist type.[1] Read too accepts the communist programme only under the condition, for him of vital importance, that even during the period of revolutionary struggle the freedom of artistic creation should not be restricted for political considerations. And he repeatedly complains, that 'even Communism, the creed of liberty and fraternity, has made the exigencies of a transitional epoch the excuse for an unnecessary and stupid form of aesthetic intolerance.'[2]

Perhaps Read does not realise that in putting forth this condition he throws a doubt upon the whole foundation of orthodox communism. But this vagueness reflects again his typically English love for synthesis by which the conflicts between a foreign political ideology and the traditional liberal form of life is overcome and adjusted in a way that follows laws of its own.

Read's political attitude has been strongly influenced by Julien Benda. Even though today he claims to have overcome this influence and to have reduced it to the right proportions, it is not difficult to see that much of his criticising attitude towards society,

---

[1] Cf. H. Straumann, 'Wird England radikal?' *Schweizerische Rundschau*, December 1936.

[2] *Surrealism*, p. 89; cf. also *Art and Society*, p. 268. Read's attitude towards communism does, however, become quite clear only in *Poetry and Anarchism*, 1938.

even of recent date, originates in the ideological sphere of Benda's *La Trahison des clercs*.[1] It is true Read has outgrown Benda's sterile intellectualism. But in fact he has not even today found a solution for his political problem, which is to define the active task of the artist in modern society.

More important, however, for a man like Read was probably the predominant intellectual situation of this period, which became for him the starting point for a new conception of art and life. More and more in the thought of the leading personalities of the time there is the tendency to throw a bridge between the fundamental antitheses: knowledge and faith, the static and the dynamic, experience and speculation, science and metaphysics. The spiritual development of one of the greatest philosophers in England today, A. N. Whitehead, may perhaps serve as an indication of the lines on which a slow retreat from the predominantly rationalist thinking of the preceding period has taken place. The turning-point is marked by the book *Science and the Modern World*, published in 1926, in which Whitehead expounds his Philosophy of the Organism.

As is proved in his essay on Descartes,[2] Read discovers in Whitehead a scheme of the universe with the preconditions for a theory of art according to which the aesthetic-intuitive act of thinking penetrates to that universal unity which remains for ever hidden to discursive reason. Artistic intuition is defined as 'the sudden realisation of the fact that an organic event, of which we are part, is in its turn the part of a greater unity, of a unity limited in time and space, formal and harmonious . . . it is, under the aspect of expression, the process of poetry. In this way poetry involves everything: it is the sense of integral unity without which, not only no poetry but no philosophy—even no religion—is ever possible.'[3] Again the idea of the fundamental identity of science and poetry appears on the scene. The reality of the universe cannot be found in the multitude of single, strictly defined existences, as it would appear to 'common sense'. To the philosopher influenced by the notion of atoms, and the theory of relativity, everything is in a state of creative flux. All is contained in all, and this interpenetration is particularly intimate in man.

Read's philosophy is ultimately pantheistic, leading to a negation of the self-willed, independent personality. This philosophy he has never expressed more clearly than in the following doctrine of intuition, itself inspired by Whitehead: 'But the world is not a

[1] cf. *Poetry and Anarchism*, pp. 43 ff.
[2] *The Sense of Glory*, pp. 56–77. [3] Ibid., p. 77.

concourse of particulars, and it may be doubted whether intuition can stop at particular things. Its range is not only immediate, but also universal. And for a concept of this wider reality we must return to Professor Whitehead. "We have to admit that the body is the organism whose states regulate our cognisance of the world. The unity of the perceptual field therefore must be a unity of bodily experience. In being aware of the bodily experience, we must thereby be aware of aspects of the whole spatio-temporal world as mirrored within the bodily life." [1]

The essence of reason, which Read has always striven for, now becomes again somewhat more distinct. It is a kind of religious, mystical power of vision. It is also the kind of insight which succeeds in bridging the gap between the data of the senses and abstract, physical theory. The auxiliary concept which helps to supersede the particular is that of the organism. The highest goal of poetry becomes the 'sense of integral unity', to feel one with the world-organism.

The place of this philosophy in the general intellectual situation of the time has never been more acutely, and also more devastatingly defined than by Wyndham Lewis, the typical representative of classical realism. 'What, finally, the contemporary intelligence,' he writes, 'does not seem to have grasped is that the whole of this movement from Bergson to the philosophers who are interpreting Relativity, is *romantic*, with all that that word conveys in its most florid, unreal, inflated, self-deceiving connotation. . . . All their thought is weighted and drugged with an intense vehement unreality.' [2]

Even if we leave aside the sneers of this master of satire at 'contemporary intelligence', there remains his right insight into the fundamentally romantic character of this movement which counts also Whitehead among its representatives. It is the same movement which has produced in poetry the modern preoccupation with consciousness. The rigid view of the universe under an unbroken naturalism fades; the glance into the interior of one's own ego promises new freedom, reality no longer consists in the merely tangible; it is 'experience in time, experience which embraces everything, the world and ourselves, a ripple, a flow, a *continuum*, a stream of consciousness.' [3] This is the path Read has chosen to

[1] *The Sense of Glory*, pp. 75 f.

[2] *Time and Western Man*, 1927, p. 186.

[3] Bernard Fehr, *Die englische Literatur der Gegenwart und die Kulturfragen unserer Zeit*, 1930, p. 41.

take, and on which only a small step was necessary to bring him to Surrealism.

Apart from these political and general intellectual motives, there must be mentioned also a personal element which determined Read to turn away from the classicist conception of art and life. The life of a civil servant which he led between the years 1919 and 1931 was in no way congenial to his artistic temperament. One is probably not far wrong in attributing the frequently strained and slightly thwarted note in his essays of that period to the material circumstances in which he found himself at that time. In all his books published after 1931 there is a fresher and more balanced element. This new freedom he owed to the professorship of Fine Arts at Edinburgh University, which he received in that year. The whole significance of this change Read describes in a letter written years later, in August 1937: 'When I left the Civil Service to become Professor of Fine Arts in Edinburgh, I felt a tremendous liberation; I had exchanged an impersonal mode of existence for a very personal one. It was largely a fictitious feeling, but I had embarked on a much more adventurous career, and had gained a liberty of expression which was not possible so long as I remained in official employment.'

The change-over from literary to art criticism is further explained by the special conditions prevailing in England in the latter field. The striking shortage of English art critics offers to anybody venturing in this direction great possibilities. For Read there was an additional consideration: in his special preoccupation with the principal questions of art he could profit more by taking in the wider field of aesthetic experience than by limiting himself to an exclusively literary orientation. The spiritual and material freedom which he had gained by getting the professorship in Edinburgh, was considerably increased by the fact that in addition he became art critic on the newly founded Radio magazine *The Listener*.

With his nearer approach to the visual arts Read begins to concentrate on the emotional aspect of art. The definition of art by means of reason is abandoned. An emotional judgment is more adequate for a painting or a piece of sculpture than for a poetic work of art. 'I grow more and more certain', Read declares, 'that it is impossible to invent ("invent is the appropriate word"), an aesthetic that holds good for all the arts. In particular, the visual or plastic arts are separated by an impassable gulf from the poetic or verbal arts. . . . The two activities are different functions in the mind, employing different faculties. Poetry proceeds from words

70

to *ideas*; plastic art proceeds from linear rhythms, harmonies of mass and colour, to *form* . . . In essence, the activities are unique.'[1] In *The Meaning of Art* Read explains the emotional nature of this plastic form: 'Form, though it can be analysed into intellectual terms like measure, balance, rhythm and harmony, is really intuitive in origin; it is not an intellectual product. It is rather emotion directed and defined, and when we describe art as "the will to form" we are not imagining an exclusively intellectual activity, but rather an exclusively instinctive one.'[2] These words, which refer to the plastic arts, foreshadow the later development of Read's aesthetics.

7. *The New Standpoint*

A comparison between the essay 'Psycho-analysis and Criticism', and that on *Form in Modern Poetry* (1932) will show in what respects Read's new standpoint differs from his former one. In order to discover Read's present attitude towards psycho-analysis and to find out what kind of literary problems he wants to solve through its medium, we have to consult also his other more recent works.

First let us turn to the essay written in 1932.

The thesis Read there puts forward is briefly as follows: art originates in the personality while the character tends to hamper artistic creation. These two psychological categories have two corresponding types of form, which Read calls organic and abstract form—a dualism which covers at the same time the two art forms, classical and romantic art: 'The correspondence of organic and abstract form with romantic and classical periods in the history of the plastic arts is obvious enough.'[3] Which means, and this is axiomatic for Read's point of view, a degradation of classical art. This is done by virtue of aesthetically diverse arguments, among which the conception of life put forward by Bergson and Whitehead is decisive: 'The transition from the organic type to the abstract always coincides with the transition from a period of stress and energy to a period of satiety and solidity. . . . And it is quite clear that the classical and romantic periods are related to each other in a "life-cycle" which is the recurring cycle of the growth, maturity and decay of a culture.'[4] Organic or romantic form ensures the highest and purest art, because 'it is the most original and most

[1] *The Listener*, 2nd April, 1930. 'Tolstoy's Theory of Art', p. 592.
[2] Loc. cit., p. 8.
[3] *Form in Modern Poetry*, p. 4.   [4] Ibid.

vital principle of poetic creation; and the distinction of modern poetry is to have recovered this principle.'[1] It is characteristic of organic form that the work of art develops only in accordance with immanent tendencies, with the effect that content and form are fused in living unity. Abstract, classical art, on the other hand, is based on the contrast between the artistic ideal of form and the subject matter, so that 'the intention of the artist is no longer related to the inherent dynanism of an inventive act.'[2]

The transition, or one may perhaps call it the conversion, to a romantic conception of art must have taken place in 1931. As late as 1930, on the 16th of April, Read writes in *The Listener*, in one of his weekly art notes: 'My own preferences are classical: that is to say, I derive most pleasure from a work of art, whether literature or painting, in which expression is achieved with some degree of formal precision. But I could never see why, though a classicist, I should be forbidden the enjoyment of romantic art.'[3] One probably does not go wrong in attributing the origins of the essay on *Form in Modern Poetry* to Read's desire, as a literary critic, to explain his new attitude by means of fundamental and theoretical principles. An empirical foundation was needed for the newly gained conviction that only organic, dynamic or romantic art was true art, and again he looked for it in psycho-analysis.

For the definition of the two conceptions personality and character Read points to Freud's treatise on *The Ego and the Id* (1923). Personality stands for the Ego. 'Freud says . . . that "in every individual there is a coherent organisation of mental processes, which we call his *ego*"; and this may serve as the preliminary definition of "personality" of which I am in search. This ego is identical with the conscious flow of our thoughts, the impressions we receive, the sensations of experience.'[4] Of paramount importance to him is the comprehensive organisation of the Ego, a fact which Freud, too, considers the main characteristic of this sector of psychic existence. ' "What most distinguishes the Ego from the Id," says Freud, "is its tendency towards a synthesis of its contents, its desire to pool and assimilate its psychic processes, motives which are altogether absent in the Id." '[5] What escapes Read in his slightly wanton way of handling psycho-analysis, is the place which the

---

[1] *Form in Modern Poetry*, p. 5.   [2] Ibid., p. 3.
[3] Loc. cit., 'Beyond Realism', p. 679.
[4] *Form in Modern Poetry*, p. 12.
[5] *Neue Folge der Vorlesungen zur Einfuehrung in die Psychoanalyse*, 1933, p. 106.

Ego occupies in the general structure of the psyche. His identification of the Ego with the 'conscious flow of thoughts' stands in contrast to the findings of the psycho-analysts.

This tendency towards synthesis, of course, corresponds entirely to the organic principle in Whitehead, and can therefore be interpreted in many ways. Like Ramon Fernandez Read calls personality the sum total of memories and sensations, which in a natural and autonomous way fuse into an inner judgment, an inner perspective. Marcel Proust, too, is called upon to confirm this identity of personality and memory. But a passage in a letter by Henry James leads further than anything Read has previously quoted. In fact, it leads him beyond the psycho-analytical explanation which he supposes he is offering. For James the creative moment appears as the elucidation of the Ego. The personality becomes conscious of itself. In an artist it possesses the gift of putting itself at a distance from its creative, synthetic faculty, to watch it, and, by acute observation, even to stimulate the creative activity. 'I think', says Read, 'in the consistent phraseology I have tried to adopt, we might say that in such a mood of creative activity, the author stands face to face with his personality. He stands fully conscious of the wavering confines of his conscious mind, an expanding and contracting, a fluctuating horizon where the light of awareness meets the darkness of oblivion: and in keeping aware of that area of light and at the same time watching the horizon for a suggestion of more light, the poet induces that new light into his consciousness; as when, at twilight, no stars are visible to a casual glance, but shine out in answer to a concentrated stare. Such lights come, of course, from the latent memory of verbal images in what Freud calls the preconscious state of the mind; or from the still obscurer state of the unconscious, in which are hidden, not only the neutral traces of repressed sensations, but also those inherited patterns which determine our instincts.'[1]

There is no evidence in psycho-analysis for this splitting up of the Ego which Read obviously undertakes in this connection. That by 'author' he does not mean the Super-ego becomes evident from the fact that he has reserved the latter concept for his definition of character. The passage in Henry James would, as it were, serve to identify Read's 'author' with the Super-ego. But this objection is of no account: one could just as well object to Read not mentioning the Libido, and the destructive instinct, or to his ignoring the Principle of Reality which after all is of great importance for the

[1] *Form in Modern Poetry*, p. 31.

synthesis of all impulses contained in the Ego. Important to note is only this: the will to form, harmony and order, which as an ideal tendency Read used to put into intentionally categorical contrast to the chaotic unconscious, this will to form he now calls organic coherence of the personality. True, at the end of his essay, he attempts to relate this coherence of personality to an ideal sphere of pure being. 'The highest poetry is inconceivable without the intuition of pure Being as well as the sense of existence.'[1] He also wants to dissociate himself from a romanticism in the narrow conventional sense. 'The romantic theory of poetry presupposes the primacy of sentiment; poetry as the direct expression of sentiment. I do not think there is anything in this essay to countenance such a theory.'[2] In stating this, however, he does not deny a wider conception of romantic form, to which the organic, synthetic, dynamic, and the hormic are more fundamental than intellect and ratio. This urge for synthesis and organisation dominates the field, from the regions of life till right up into the regions of the spirit. But it is in the personality that it finds its purest expression. In this aesthetic basing itself on Proust, McDougall, Freud, Bergson, Whitehead and Croce there is a separating gulf between the three realms, of life, soul and spirit. Life and spirit are not identical. But mutually elucidating each other, as they do, they must be thought of as coexistent.

Let us now turn to Read's definition of the character. While by personality he understands the free play of psychic impulses, regulated only by a will to organisation and inner harmony, he conceives character as a fixation of that natural flow, a surrender of the inner organisation for the sake of external legality. In the language of psycho-analysis his arguments are as follows: 'Character can be explained as a disposition in the individual due to the repression of certain impulses which would otherwise be present in the personality. Character, which has always such a positive aspect, is really the result of certain fixities or negations imposed on the flow of consciousness. A flood only gains character and direction when it is confined between banks.'[3] His views are expressed even more clearly in the following sentence: 'But speaking of the restricted, the too limited notion of personality in Corneille, he (Fernandez) gives us a perfect description of character—he describes it as "the tragic conformity of man to his definition"—Freud would say "to his ego-ideal".'[4] Read here deviates from psycho-analysis to an

---

[1] *Form in Modern Poetry*, p. 78.   [2] Ibid.
[3] Ibid., p. 13.   [4] Ibid., p. 24.

extent he himself does perhaps not realise. He intermingles ontogenetical and phylogenetical ways of thought. In the same way as in the history of art, where a period of organic form is followed by a period of abstraction, personality is superseded and displaced by character. The life of the psyche, formerly obeying an inner principle of form, now conforms to an outside force, to an external law. 'Character, in short, is an impersonal ideal which the individual selects and to which he sacrifices all other claims, especially those of the sentiments or emotions.'[1] According to Freud, however, the Ego is coexistent with the Super-ego, and will not be displaced by it; even in the romantic artist Ego and Super-ego are both active at the same time. The state of tension, natural between the two, is of great aesthetic effectiveness. The passage in Henry James's letter which Read quotes could no doubt be much better interpreted in accordance with this theory. James writes: 'What really happens is that the closer I get to the problem of the application of it in any particular case the more I get *into* that application, so that the more doubts and torments fall away from me, the more I know where I am, the more everything spreads and shines and draws me on and I'm justified of my logic and my passion.'[2] Freud has assigned to the Super-ego the function of an ideal. The inspiration described by James obviously appears as the fulfilment of the artistic ideal raised by the Super-ego. In this way the ecstasy of creative enjoyment pervading the whole of this passage is actually brought about by the release of the tension between Ego and Super-ego. Read falsely believes that the Super-ego could only dictate moral imperatives, while in fact—especially in the artist—it can just as well state aesthetic ideals. Quite possibly Read's onesidedness in judging the function of character has to do with his vehement anti-puritanism which makes him smell the devil in person in anything that bears the least resemblance to a forced moralistic order.

Five years later this theory of art, first developed in 1932, receives a modification of no small importance, in the far-reaching book *Art and Society*. In this work Read shows a greater readiness to acknowledge the influence of the time factor in all art as well as a stricter adherence to the principles of psycho-analysis. The main points, however, are the same. The creative impulse issues from the unconscious. On its way to formal completion it is transformed by the various organising mechanisms of the Ego. These mechanisms are: regression, censure, transference, condensation, displacement. The Super-ego represents the claims of society and its collective

[1] *Form in Modern Poetry*, p. 18.   [2] Ibid., p. 30.

ideals. In giving way to these claims art becomes impure. 'In certain ages society has made the artist an exponent of the moral and ideal emanations of the Super-ego, and art has thus become the handmaid of religion or morality or social ideology. In that further process art, as art, has always suffered—simply because in such a case the message will always appear more important, more insistent, than the mode of conveyance, and men will forget that in art it is only the mode which matters. But by the mode we mean more than the externals of beauty; we mean above all the driving energy, the uprush of forces from the well of the unconscious.'[1] The essence of art no longer consists in the pure harmony of unconscious forces and ideal form, as Read used to maintain. The psychic forces propagating ideals are inartistic, and even pernicious. A work of art is the more poetical the more it leaves the categories of reason. 'Certain of the dream-thoughts have been condensed into images or symbols, whose latent significance resists any analysis, but which, nevertheless, *and perhaps precisely on that account,* have extreme poetic force.'[2] The classical-realistic postulates of order, harmony, rhythm and symmetry are abandoned. Their place is taken by the ideas of a supreme, autonomous force of creation. Reality is dethroned, and super-reality is now regarded as the aesthetically dominant factor. This is the end of a logical development that took Read from his ideas as expressed in *Form in Modern Poetry* in a straight line to the exclusive recognition of the forces of the Ego.

It remains to be said that fundamentally it makes no great difference whether these forces are thought to be dwelling in the personality or in the Unconscious. In both cases, what carries the day, is a super-individual, collective and therefore conventional reality. What is expressed in art is not some value wholly different from reality, or as in Surrealism from super-reality. For such value there would be no room in idealistic-empirical philosophy. The notion of reality is now by Read simply enlarged by the recognition of that 'something-more-than-conscious naturalism, which encompasses all our actions.'[3] But the conception of a reality that has its intuitive reflection in art is never really got rid of.

[1] Loc. cit., p. 204. [2] *Surrealism*, p. 76.
[3] Ibid., p. 79.

8. Summary

The development of Read's psychology of literature as it has been traced in these pages, can be condensed into five major points.

1. The attempt to establish a doctrine of values has been abandoned. Not only the notion of 'social validity', but also the other elements of Jung's psychology of types are dropped. Aesthetic value no longer rests on a supposed affinity between the work of art and the ideal aspirations of collectivity. The greatness of a genius, too, can no longer be measured on these lines. On the contrary, spontaneous energy itself is the only value. The distinction between extraversion and introversion, which served Read still in 1925 as a means of defining the classical and the romantic, has in its present doctrine lost its meaning. For the term 'classical art' itself is for this doctrine altogether a *contradictio in adiecto*.

2. The conception of an 'ideal or affective tendency' has undergone a complete transformation. Its place is taken by the organising force of the ego, a notion completely different from it, both in character and in function. The ideal tendency could be likened to an artist's peculiar weapon with which he conquered the instincts endangering his spiritual life. But in Read's later conception, the synthetic tendency of the ego is not a prerogative of the artist, but exists also in the ordinary person. The difference is only that the artist need not suppress these instincts, but tries to express them in all their vividness. '(The artist) does not eliminate any element which is a contribution from internal sources of excitation: *his* purpose (as opposed to that of the ordinary person) is precisely to introduce such elements, and so disturb the even and orderly surface of the ordinary man's conception of reality by the introduction of forces from that deeper level of being which we call the id.'[1] The formerly strongly felt struggle between reason and emotion has forthwith been decided in favour of emotion. The danger of a neurosis does not seem so terrible any longer; on the contrary, abnormal states of mind are sought for and cultivated. Can one from that perhaps draw the conclusion that in Read himself the violence and emotion of his younger years has given way to greater calmness? That the renunciation of reason is felt by him more as a liberation than as dangerous subjectivism?

3. To the debunking of the ideal tendency corresponds a higher view of emotion. Earlier Read used to define poetry as a spiritual

[1] *Art and Society*, p. 227.

antithesis of reality; in which process the poet was playing rather a passive part. Reality dictated to him its laws: they were the laws of reason derived from experience. Poetry was 'but the precise statement of such abstractions as the poet derives from his experience. Perhaps, in the scholastic sense, it is the poetry of universals.'[1]

And while he maintained as late as 1932 that the motives and images rising from the unconscious can be raised to the rank of a work of art only by the harmonising and idealising influence of the ego, he now considers it the highest aim to give these motives direct expression. Once a surrealist poem has pushed its way upwards into consciousness—following the same laws by which dreams are produced—the task left to the ideal tendency is really very poor and inartistic: 'Then, to disguise any gaps or incoherency, the conscious mind of the poet has worked over the poem, and given it that smooth façade which is generally demanded by the literary conventions of an age, and which in any case make for ease of communication.'[2] And here is another quotation which might serve to demonstrate Read's abandonment of a reality, external in spite of being spiritual, for the sake of an inner reality, more comprehensive because embracing also the unconscious life of the instincts. Read had admired earlier on in Donne 'a mind poised at the exact turn of the course of philosophy—drawing his inspiration right back from scholastic sources, and yet at the same time eagerly surveying the new future promised by the science of Copernicus and Galileo.'[3]

Today (he has come to believe), the poet no longer draws his inspiration from a reality lit up by reason; he believes in the existence of reason in a wider sense, a reason which covers also the most obscure corners of the mind.

4. What is Read's attitude towards psychology in the various phases of his development? His faith in psycho-analysis has never faltered. On the other hand he has never in any of his works critically examined the theoretic, scientific or philosophic principles of this psychology. He never seems to have gone deeper into the teachings of those psychologists and philosophers who adhere to a fundamentally different conception, like Spinoza, Locke, the psychology of associations, Darwin and behaviourism. His essay on Descartes becomes to him only a pretext for developing an entirely uncartesian concept of intuition.[4] Read's critical efforts in this field are confined to supplementing psycho-analysis metaphorically 'from

[1] *Reason and Romanticism*, p. 56.   [2] *Surrealism*, p. 76.
[3] *Reason and Romanticism*, p. 43.
[4] *The Sense of Glory*, pp. 58–77.

above'. In this he often finds surprising confirmation in thinkers like Vico, Shelley, Blake, Coleridge, Herder, Bergson and Whitehead—and one cannot but admire his felicitous gift for hitting upon the right text. His grasp of the idealistic philosophers is more limited. He quotes Plato as a far-sighted theoretician of modern abstract art.[1] His acquaintance with and appreciation of Thomism is derived from Jacques Maritain, one-time disciple of Bergson. With Hegel and Croce Read agrees only with strong reservations. From this one-sidedness of interest and appreciation one most come to the conclusion that in his theoretical thought Read is more akin to those representatives of a dionysian conception of mind, which are described by W. McDougall in his essay on 'The present Chaos in Psychology', and among which are counted also Freud and his followers.[2]

5. It would however be wrong to deduce from this course of development that Read is a pure Romantic who at last, in his thirty-seventh year of life, threw off his classical prejudices. It is more true to think of him as one of those contradictory personalities who attain to a balance or synthesis of their inner dialectic only very rarely and never for long. The 'classicism' which he stands for in the twenties is as little genuine and conceptually pure as that of his friend T. S. Eliot. They both had set themselves the task of reconciling a romantic inclination with the claims of reason. The solution Eliot arrived at was to clothe his romantic aspirations in forms that —once pulsating and striving for the infinite—now consummate a tradition in the rigidity of an impersonal grandeur. In all fields, not only in that of literature, Eliot succumbs to the charm of perfected forms, to the historically grown and purified tradition. Read, on the other hand, looks for a different solution. It is certain that, under the influence of Eliot he has approached an ideal of art which wants to combine highest intensity of feeling with the most lucid thought. A tendency to spiritual precision and lucidity of expression was also the effect produced on him by an author like Julien Benda, of whose works Read has read, as he himself admits, practically everything that was published between 1920 and 1930.

The classicist elements we noted in his thought before 1930 can most probably be in part ascribed to these influences. Otherwise they are effects of his already mentioned constitutional longing for order and simplicity. The true balance, however, between these

[1] *Art Now*, pp. 101 f.

[2] *Journal of Philosophical Studies*, vol. v, 1930, quoted by R. Metz, loc. cit.

'appollinic' tendencies and his fundamentally romantic sensibility is found by way of the aesthetic experience, and in particular through the work of art itself. In creative imagination Read experiences a reality that is clear and ordered as well as dynamic. Read's definition of reason and intuition is only an attempt to apply to this experience a rational formula, an attempt which—like that of I. A. Richards—does not amount to more than giving a merely intuitive and explanatory description of the 'fact of mind'.

(Translated by Léonie Cohn)

ROBERT MELVILLE

THE FIRST SIXTY-SIX PAGES OF
THE GREEN CHILD

The last sentence on page 66 closes the first section of *The Green Child*, and brings to a fitting conclusion one of the most perfect narratives in the English language.

Strictly speaking, the title of the novel belongs only to this section. Sally, the Green Child, does not appear at all in the second part, which is the story of Olivero's life before their meeting, and in the third part her name is changed to Siloën and attached to one of the slightly nauseating inhabitants of a subterranean world: these two sections, the story of President Olivero and the study of the green people, are descriptions of Utopias—a patronising Utopia for masses and a puritanical, quasi-intellectual one for individuals. It seems probable that the two distinct Oliveros who appear in them are projections of that Silver Knight who figured in Read's adolescent day-dreams, 'riding to quixotic combats, attaining a blinding and indefinable glory',[1] and represent two experimentally isolated aspects of the personality of their creator; so the stories in which they appear could be considered as parts of an uncentred composition (having a not too remote analogy in Paul Klee's *Le Temps et les Plantes*), as studies of coexistent aspects of Olivero artificially developed as successive actions, if only the story which gives the book its title were equally unqualified by complex emotional experience. As it is, although they have been attached to this story with admirable ingenuity the attachment has no formal necessity.

I prefer, then, to consider the first 66 pages of *The Green Child* as a complete work, and to confine my attention to these pages, which tell of Olivero's return to his native village, of his meeting with the Green Child in dramatic circumstances, of the Green Child's release from thirty years of cruel captivity, and of their disappearance together when 'hand in hand they sank below the surface of the pool.' I am giving this story the title of the novel, but between inverted commas instead of in italics.

Its motif is a well-chosen improbability, and the descriptions of

---

[1] *Annals of Innocence and Experience*, Faber & Faber, 1940.

natural phenomena and psychological states which permeate the unfolding of the narrative are so strictly relevant that we are made to feel the reality of the unexplainable and the credibility of the Green Child herself. There are no explanations, the story has no significance exterior to itself and it does not invite us to speculate upon its symbolism. The Green Child is as clearly a water nymph as the Queen of Spades is the Evil Eye, in Pushkin's story; we need to know no more than that. And it is pleasant to be able to acknowledge, after having had a frustrated desire to bring his name into almost everything I have written, that the mention of Pushkin here is made under the compulsion of the rare quality of Herbert Read's story, for in its perfection as pure narrative, in its fascination as a thing in itself, in the transparent yet inimitable logic of its construction it is the equal of the finest of all Pushkin's stories.

Such stories are persistently re-read primarily for the beauty of their composition, and for this reason they must be sealed, there must be no outlets through which they can mingle with our experience; in their circumstantiality they may bear only the merest fortuitous resemblance to the real world; they must be without any shadow of indecision or equivocation; they must be distinct and apart from us, absolute and indisputable. So in 'The Green Child', as in *The Queen of Spades*, the potentialities of the characters are completely used up by the action, and the responsibility of rendering them finally hermetic is laid upon the concluding sentences. Pushkin's old princess, who held the secret of the cards, is dead, Hermann of the Engineers has gone insane and will repeat forever, 'Three, seven, ace! Three, seven, queen!' and Lizaveta Ivanovna lives in felicity with 'a very agreeable young man', arousing neither our curiosity nor our scepticism. In the Read story, we have the equally satisfying 'evidence of our senses' that Kneeshaw, the tormentor of the Green Child, is floating face-upwards in the stream—and the last exultant sentence plunges Sally and Olivero into the oblivion of the waters to assure us that their hands will never be unclasped. The little Yorkshire village, with its stream, its railway station, tannery and two mills, is a closed garden.

A sequel to either story is unthinkable. That Read should have attempted one has a psychological interest which I do not wish to exploit; I am concerned with what effect it may have had upon 'The Green Child', and curiously enough it would appear to be beneficial, for the suppression of any reference to the Green Child's origin, which might have clouded our perception of her true identity, may be due in part to the fact that Read had the sub-terranean sequel in mind.

There is a phrase on page 64 inserted in the interests of the South American Utopia ('. . . and during that time Olivero told the Green Child the story of his life, more or less as it is related on another page.') which is a minute enough blemish certainly, but which does not cease to be disquieting as a sign that we are going to be taken behind the scenes. Fortunately, the other references to this Utopia have been perfectly assimilated. The bold opening, for instance, which tells us that the president of a South American state arranged his own assassination so that he could return to the English village where he spent his childhood, obtains for Olivero a character of decision, a romantic background and a long journey home which manage to give his meeting with the Green Child a magical inevitability quite remote from the clumsy machinery of coinci-dence which turns a 'realistic' novel such as *Two on a Tower* into a farce.

'The Green Child' is based upon a folk tale entitled *The Green Children*, which Read quotes in his chapter on Fantasy in *English Prose Style*,[1] and because it seems to me that the nature of the modifications and extensions made by Read in the course of trans-forming this material into a specific dramatic episode needs to be followed in some detail if we are to appreciate the superb part played by the critical intelligence, I reproduce it here in its entirety.

'At St. Mary's of the Wolf-pits in Suffolk, a boy and his sister were found by the inhabitants of that place near the mouth of a pit which is there, who had the form of all their limbs like to those of other men, but they differed in the colour of their skin from all the people of our habitable world; for the whole surface of their skin was tinged of a green colour. No one could understand their speech. When they were brought as curiosities to the house of a certain knight, Sir Richard de Caine, at Wikes, they wept bitterly. Bread and other victuals were set before them, but they would touch none of them, though they were tormented by great hunger, as the girl afterwards acknowledged. At length, when some beans just cut, with their stalks, were brought into the house, they made signs, with great avidity, that they should be given to them. When they were brought, they opened the stalks instead of the pods, thinking the beans were in the hollow of them; but not finding them there, they began to weep anew. When those who were present saw this, they opened the pods, and showed them the naked beans. They fed

[1] Bell, 1928.

on these with great delight, and for a long time tasted no other food. The boy however was always languid and depressed, and he died within a short time. The girl enjoyed continual good health, and becoming accustomed to various kinds of food, lost completely that green colour, and gradually recovered the sanguine habit of her entire body. She was afterwards regenerated by the laver of holy baptism, and lived for many years in the service of that knight (as I have frequently heard from him and his family), and was rather loose and wanton in her conduct. Being frequently asked about the people of her country, she asserted that the inhabitants, and all they had in that country, were of a green colour; and that they saw no sun, but enjoyed a degree of light like what is after sunset. Being asked how she came into this country with the aforesaid boy, she replied, that as they were following their flocks they came to a certain cavern, on entering which they heard a delightful sound of bells; ravished by whose sweetness, they went for a long time wandering on through the cavern until they came to its mouth. When they came out of it, they were struck senseless by the excessive light of the sun, and the unusual temperature of the air; and thus they lay for a long time. Being terrified by the noise of those who came on them, they wished to fly, but they could not find the entrance of the cavern before they were caught.'

The folk tale appears to refer in time to the middle ages, but only the reference to the 'house of a certain knight, Sir Richard de Caine, at Wikes,' gives this impression, and the period remains essentially indeterminate. Read mentions 1861 as the year in which the events of his story took place, but gives only a tenuous impression of the nineteenth century, and the effect achieved is of a distilled and leisurely contemporaneity. The precise dating, like the careful recording of the duration of the several movements of the action, is a contribution to the simulation of circumstantiality, and is as much an abstraction as the letter R in one of Paul Klee's landscapes; Klee had partly to abstract his landscape to enable it to assimilate the alphabetical intrusion, and Read is able to give an exact date without fear of setting his story emphatically in the past because he too has partly abstracted his landscape and his people, and has secured thereby an effect not of distance in time but of distance in space, of a kind which is associated with the effect of remoteness and intensified definition obtained through a diminishing-glass.

A passage in *The Meaning of Art*[1] may help me to indicate one of the sources of that abstract quality in 'The Green Child' which

[1] Faber & Faber, 1931.

can convey by seeming pedantries an air of elegance and natural order: the passage occurs when Read is about to define the quality of modern landscape painting: 'In the first place, I would say that it has nothing to do with the quasi-scientific interest in the morphology[1] of rocks and plants which inspired the only possible predecessor of Patinir in this branch of art—Leonardo da Vinci.' Leonardo, in his studies of plants abstracted from their habitat reproduces their delicate living curves with exactitude and follows their complex interweavings with an inordinate effort of will yet with a spontaneous vitality and elegance of line, and our response to his specimens is a kind of intellectual exhilaration. Read, too, is able to compel this kind of response because he persistently gives us the 'morphology' of a situation; he abstracts a situation from its emotional ambience but presents the inter-relationship of the components with such fidelity that the overtones arise in the reader's mind by involuntary deduction. The following extract from a description of a fight between Olivero and Kneeshaw is a simple instance—there are others which have an astoundingly lucid intricacy.

'Olivero struggled and succeeded in getting his right arm free and this he pressed palm upwards, with all his force against Kneeshaw's chin, hoping to make him release his grip. But he felt himself being lifted off the ground in spite of all his efforts. Kneeshaw tried to turn with his burthen, and Olivero seized the opportunity, when his opponent's balance was all on one leg, of suddenly hurling his weight forward, kicking backwards against the wall of the mill. Kneeshaw staggered and fell across the platform. His head hung over the pit, but he still gripped Olivero like a snake. Olivero spread out his legs to guard against being turned over, and found a buttress for each foot, one against the wall of the mill, the other against the chute. It would be practically impossible for the strongest man to overturn him. With his disengaged hand he was still pressing back the hard foul chin of Kneeshaw, and now he pressed with all his force. He knew that in this way he could break his neck, but he did not wish to go to such an extremity.'

It is interesting to compare this with a Hemingway piece:

'It wasn't about anything, something about making punch, and then we started fighting and I slipped and he had me down kneeling on my chest and choking me with both hands like he was trying to kill me and all the time I was trying to get the knife out of my pocket to cut him loose. Everybody was too drunk to pull him off

[1] Klee's *Le Temps et les Plantes* is an example of fantastic morphology.

me. He was choking me and hammering my head on the floor and I got the knife out and opened it up; and I cut the muscle right across his arm and he let go of me. He couldn't have held on if he wanted to.'[1]

Hemingway's blurred factualism reproduces much more vividly than Read's passage the proximity and breathlessness, the moil, the ugly violence, but the actual moves of the antagonists are not clearly defined. Read's graph of the contest presents with extreme clarity the changes of position and posture which give Olivero the upper hand, and the sum of these moves generates the notion of murder. Read keeps his distance and achieves sharper definition.[2]

All the same, Read's clear, economical style is more akin to that of Hemingway's sportsman's sketches than to any other twentieth-century writing. There is a striking resemblance between the description of Olivero's walk along the bank of the stream and Hemingway's wonderful evocation of a North American river in *In Our Time*. The resemblance is not distinctly to be found in the texture of the writing for Read constructs a longer sentence and eschews Hemingway's excessive use of conjunctions, but both writers are distinguished by the cool, sharp, homesick eye and the gift of progression, and both can claim stylistic descent from Defoe. But whereas Hemingway has a forthrightness and an inherently objective vision which makes him almost 'the modern Defoe' Read's relationship to Defoe is not so simply a matter of

[1] *Winner Take Nothing*, Cape, 1934.

[2] In one of his articles for *The Listener* (27th May, 1936) he invents a clear, bold, wholly delightful visual image to bring sharply into focus the world-wide reputation of Picasso. 'We can imagine an actual triumph: the streets adorned with garlands, everyone in carnival dress, shouts of *Io triumphe*! At the head of the procession, instead of a senate, we might place the dealers—Messieurs Vollard and Kahnweiler, the brothers Rosenberg, Pierre Colle and Pierre Loeb, Mr. Zwemmer and Mr Mayor. Instead of the trumpeters would come the critics, led by Monsieur Zervos, the authors of the twenty books on Picasso, the writers of the hundred essays on Picasso. For trophies there would be paintings, statues and models by the thousand imitators of Picasso. Prominent among the victims destined for sacrifice would be a living representation of Venus, and the prisoners would, of course, include all the members of the Royal Academy and the Académie Française. Picasso's chariot might still be drawn by the traditional four bulls; laurels would sit well on his head, but instead of a sceptre he would hold a brush in his hand, and his palette would be held by a moneylender to remind him in the midst of his glory that he was a mortal man. He would be followed by an international army of admirers, and after the feast there would be a bull-fight for Picasso to paint.'

affinity; his is not by any means a return to Defoe's documentary style, but is rather an aftermath of that style's complex and passionate flowering in *Wuthering Heights*, the heat gone and its traces calcined.

In the folk tale the girl eventually loses her green colour, but not, of course, in Read's story, and he describes her distinctive colouring in a lovely passage:

'The skin was not white, but a faint green shade, the colour of a duck's egg. It was, moreover, an unusually transparent tegument, and through its pallor the branches spread, not blue and scarlet, but vivid green and golden. The nails were pale blue, very like a blackbird's egg-shell. The faint emanation of odour from her flesh was sweet and a little heavy, like the scent of violets.'

Later, changes of colour and other manifestations under certain emotional states are exquisitely observed.

'Anger and astonishment she did not show by any vocal or facial expression, but in a trembling of the limbs and a clouding of her translucent flesh; joy was expressed by an increased radiance of flesh, by a bright onyx flame in her eyes, and by a laughter which was a soft crooning sound at the base of her throat. Sorrow, like affection, she did not seem to know, but fear and repugnance produced that blanching or etiolation of the flesh which was the effect of depriving her of the sunlight, but produced it suddenly like an inverse blush.'

Read has not dispensed here with what Maurras calls the 'carnal flavour' of words, but it will be noticed that in each of these two descriptions a somewhat pedantically worded phrase—'It was, moreover, an unusually transparent tegument', 'Anger and astonishment she did not show by any vocal or facial expression'—has the effect of putting a decent distance between the describer and the described, and produces even a faint frigidity. This frigidity in the style is like an emanation from the Green Child herself, who shrank from the heat of a human body and was never known to show affection for human being or animal.

The substance of the Green Child is imaginary, for she is a naiad, the tutelary spirit of the stream which plays so important a part in the story, and there is a simple though unemphatic allegorical reason for her appearance in the village on the same day that Olivero leaves it, and for the setting of her thirty years of captivity in the middle of the nineteenth century. The Industrial Revolution, as represented by the ignorance and destructiveness of Kneeshaw, has driven away the Poet, in the person of Olivero. Olivero's presidency of a South American state, in the interval between his departure and return, can be considered as a symbol of ascendancy in another order of reality, so that when he comes back for a day and a night to find the naiad in much the same plight as those angels of Rilke's who had forgotten how to fly and 'were like heavy birds, ruined birds',[1] he is powerful enough to restore her dignity and freedom and accompany her into the stream, for his return is equivalent to a poetic inspiration in which past glory is evoked with the force of a resurrection.

Knowing that she is a water nymph, we are not surprised that the Green Child, despite her delicately feminine appearance, is sexless, and it is one of the triumphs of Read's narrative skill that Kneeshaw's insensitiveness to this fact provides her with a concrete reality. The folk tale remarks of the girl that she was 'rather loose and wanton in her conduct', and since we are unable to drain this remark of sexual meaning it is completely out of character with the Green Child. But it is a detail which has been kept alive in Read's story by its transference to the hopes and desires of Kneeshaw. 'He could not conceive that anything so feminine (and therefore so strongly attractive to his masculinity) could be without what we in the learned world call sexual characteristics, and the blind motive of all the attention he devoted to the Green Child had no other origin.' There was 'the possibility of discovering in her a different mode of love'. She never ceased to fascinate him, but after some years, incited by his unappeased desires, he began to torment her.

The torment to which she is being subjected when Olivero returns has its foundation in one of her peculiarities, which in its turn derives from a peculiarity of the green children in the folk story. The green children refused the various foods that were brought to them and would eat only raw beans; the Green Child was avid 'only of hazel-nuts, sweet-briar and water-cress, and all kinds of mushrooms and toadstools.' She had a horror of meat. Out of this peculiarity arises the most dramatic and cunningly devised scene in the narrative. Suddenly, in a set-piece as yet unmodified by explanation, we are confronted by pure melodrama.

'On a bare table to the right lay the lamb; its throat had been cut and was bleeding into a large bowl, over the edge of which its head hung pathetically. In the middle of the room the man stood, drawing back the head of a woman by the hair and compelling her to drink from a cup which he held in his hand. So much was clear at a glance; then Olivero noticed that the woman, who was extraordinarily frail

[1] E. M. Butler, *Rainer Maria Rilke*, Cambridge, 1941.

and pallid, was bound by a rope to the chair in which she was seated, and that her expression was one of concentrated terror as she struggled to refuse the proffered cup. The blood which she was being forced to drink dribbled down each side of her mouth and fell in bright stains down the front of her white dress. The light came from a paraffin-lamp, whose golden globe swung impassively above this scene of terror.'

The eucharistic symbolism of the blood of the lamb with which Kneeshaw torments the Green Child confirms her pagan identity; it is Read's comment upon the statement in the folk tale that the girl was 'regenerated by the laver of holy baptism'.

After contemplating this scene for a few moments, Olivero makes a move which abruptly introduces an element of farce: ' . . . he hurled himself into the room, legs foremost as he had observed the man do; but, unfortunately, as he clung to the sash of the window to raise himself and twist his body round, the sash descended and left him in an incongruous position, the upper half of his body outside the window, his legs waving wildly inside the room.'

The introduction of this new element has the effect of maintaining and augmenting the tableau which was framed by the window at the same time that the 'tyranny of the frame' is broken, and a kind of dynamic suspension of activity is achieved which removes the necessity for further physical violence. The initial struggle between Olivero and Kneeshaw begins immediately, but on another plane, in a curious atmosphere of predestination and psychological subtlety for which the macabre and complex visual image has prepared us.

In *English Prose Style* Read says, 'there is a natural tendency . . . for the ballad and folk tale to develop a clear objective narrative, but a narrative encumbered by odd inconsequential but startlingly vivid and concrete details,' and of *The Green Children* in particular, 'this is the norm to which all types of fantasy should conform. The only difference is, that in the conscious literary inventions with which we are nowadays concerned, the will or intention of the writer has to take the part of the age-long and impersonal forces of folk tradition.' But Read, in supplementing these forces with the forces of a personal vision, has achieved something radically different in kind from *The Green Children*. The 'startlingly vivid and concrete details' are multiplied and refined, but the literary conscience which conserves them and which seeks above all else to develop anew 'a clear and objective narrative' so orders and articulates these details that their inconsequentialness is expunged. When Olivero submerges his wrist finally to assure himself that the stream is flowing in reverse, the act and the small, cold shock are premonitory; the spell has been cast and the enchantment begins; from that point he follows a course of action which leads irrevocably to death by drowning. Kneeshaw and Olivero both meet their fate in the stream, but for one it is reprobation and for the other it is election. The Green Child and Olivero, denied the sweetest sport of shepherds, are the last, austere children of pastoral.

Read has said (again, in *English Prose Style*) 'Poetry alone is creative. The art of prose is not creative, but constructive or logical.' *The Green Child* is pre-eminently a construction, yet in essence it is a poetical achievement, and of a kind which Read himself has admirably described. It is ' . . . the vision of an unknown garden, embedded in glass, clear but unattainable. Vision without meaning, concrete, synthetic, but held in suspense, contemplated without question.'[1]

[1] *In Defence of Shelley and Other Essays,* Heinemann, 1936.

H. W. HÄUSERMANN

HERBERT READ'S POETRY

'What I mean by classical verse, then, is this. That even in the most imaginative flights there is always a holding back, a reservation. The classical poet never forgets this finiteness, this limit of man. He remembers always that he is mixed up with earth. He may jump, but he always returns back; he never flies away into the circumambient gas.'

Speculations, pp. 119–120, T. E. HULME

1. Eclogues (1914–1918)

Herbert Read acknowledged his early adherence to the Imagist school of poetry in an article on 'The Present State of Poetry' published in 1939. He writes:
'We were in revolt, just before the War, against certain tame conventions which Hopkins (though we did not then know it), had described as Parnassian—a poeticism, or poetry derived from poetry, which Bridges represented at its best, Alfred Noyes at its worst. . . . The new impetus came from a very unpoetic source—the logical and cynical mind of T. E. Hulme; and from a very un-English direction—the America of Ezra Pound, behind which, however, was the France of Rémy de Gourmont, Edouard Dujardin, and, still farther removed, the France of Rimbaud and Laforgue'[1]).

He then affirms that 'the new ideal, which we called Imagism, was what we can now recognise as the eternal aesthetic ideal—an ideal of form, indifferent to the nature of the subject-matter'. Precision and vitality of image, crystalline objectivity, sincerity of feeling, exactness of expression, these were the qualities aimed at by the Imagists. Moreover, they tried to combine freshness of inspiration with formal perfection. Thus, intuitive, even automatic composition should result in verse of classical texture. It was to be the opposite of loose, straggling, incoherent verse.

Not all of the twenty 'Eclogues' published in Read's *Poems* 1914-1934 (Faber & Faber, 1935) fulfil these conditions. Some of them are spoilt by an adolescent *Weltschmerz* incompatible with objectivity. Repeated comparisons of the poet's heart with a limp yellow worm-eaten leaf falling to the wet earth betray not only immaturity of

---

[1] *The Kenyon Review* (Quarterly, Gambier, O.). Autumn, 1939, p. 359.

mind but also certain literary influences: the feeling that one's soul is like a tenuous membrane or like the surface of a lake rippled by the slightest breeze is characteristic of those young poets who, during and just after the War, studied the French symbolists and felt only contempt for the more realistic aspects of Georgianism.[1] To be weary of life, of the world and of men, to be merely a sensitive and passive mirror of nature—that is the 'literary' and immature element in Read's early Imagist verse. He has rightly excluded these eclogues from his recent collection of *Thirty-five Poems* (Faber & Faber, 1940).

The remaining 'Eclogues' fall into two classes. There are those which achieve a maximum of objectivity: pure evocations of sense impressions, hard dry statements.[2] 'Childhood' and 'On the Heath' are examples of this style. These poems foreshadow Read's later work as an art critic: as 'the primary nature of aesthetic appreciation is purely sensual, and a natural biological function',[3] they show evidence of Read's special sensibility.

Most of Read's 'Eclogues', however, and in our opinion the best, are filled with a dark passionate emotion, a Lawrentian impulse centred in the body. His nature poetry leads up to the apprehension of something far more deeply interfused, but not to a refined pantheism like that of Wordsworth's poetry. Read's emotion expands in the feeling of nearness to the earth, in the hidden beauty of pine woods, of the homely valley under the wood-topped hills. This animal sense of oneness with the earth is beautifully expressed in the first section of that strange poem, 'The Sorrow of Unicume': a darkly sexual emotion, the pleasure and pain of passion, is combined with the peasant's communion with his land. The poem ends significantly with a prayer for victory over the emotional disturbance:

> 'White flower unfeeling,
> you star the mould:
> evolvèd calmness,
> my heart enfold.'

[1] All references to Read's poems, unless otherwise stated, are from the *Poems 1914–1934*. See 'Meditation of a Lover at Daybreak', 'The Orchard', 'Curfew', and section III of 'The Sorrow of Unicume'. For an ironical portrait of such a young poet see Aldous Huxley, *Crome Yellow*, 1921. (Phoenix Library, pp. 278 f.)

[2] The Imagists' use of hard dry statement derives, not from the Symbolists, but from Gautier and Rimbaud, although Claudel and Kahn, too, prefer direct statement to indirect suggestion. See Réne Taupin, *L'influence du Symbolisme français sur la poésie américaine (de 1910 a 1920)*, Thèse, Paris, 1929, pp. 104, 150–155.

[3] See Herbert Read, *Art and Industry*, Faber & Faber, 1934, p. 127.

This desire for calmness and control of emotion coincided with the principal tenet of Imagism. It gave T. E. Hulme his definition of classicism with its characteristic effects of hardness and dryness, and it enabled Eliot to associate himself with Pound's 'rebellion against the romantic tradition which insists that a poet should be continu-ally inspired'.[1] Read's striving after 'evolvèd calmness' springs, how-ever, less from aesthetic theories than from the deepest tendencies of his race. We know that he was born on a farm near Kirbymoor-side, in the North Riding of Yorkshire, where 'we could see around us the misty hills, the Moors to the norths, the Wolds to the south, meeting dimly in the east where they were more distant'.[2] He lived at the farm until he was nine. When his father died, he was sent to a boarding-school at Halifax. With Wordsworth the poet shares therefore not only similar memories of childhood in the North of England but also an outstanding characteristic of Yorkshiremen. Read himself describes this trait in his discussion of Wordsworth's ancestry:

'Yorkshiremen are imaginative, like all northmen, but a matter-of-factness, a strong sense of objectivity, a faculty for vivid visualisa-tion, keep them from being profoundly mystical. . . . But their most extraordinary characteristic—a characteristic with which in the process of time they have leavened almost the entire English race—is their capacity for masking their emotions. . . . Passion, of course, does blaze from many a poem of Wordsworth's; but not the direct passion of profane love, not even the direct passion of sacred love, but passion transmuted into impersonal things—rocks, and stones, and trees.'[3]

All that applies also to Read himself—with one reservation. The word 'mask' implies insincerity, moral repression or inhibition. It implies a persistence of excessive, anti-social passion under the cover of formal control. Read's desire for 'evolvèd calmness' does not spring from Puritanical motives such as inspire certain poems of Wordsworth.[4] These motives destroy the original passion, whereas Read wishes his poetry to achieve a natural and logical 'evolution' of this passion until it has reached the calm objectivity of a work of art. His longer poem, 'The Analysis of Love', is a perfect example

[1] See Eliot's introduction to Ezra Pound, *Selected Poems*, Faber & Faber, 1928, p. xx.

[2] Herbert Read, *The Innocent Eye*, Faber & Faber, 1933, p. 9.

[3] Herbert Read, *Wordsworth, The Clark Lectures, 1929–1930*. First published 1930. Second edition: Cape, 1932, pp. 43 f.

[4] See Read's book on Wordsworth, pp. 118, 214–218.

of this process of the sublimation of emotion towards the 'evolvèd calmness' of art.

2. War Poems (1916–1932)

It appears that the short pieces collected under the title of 'The Scene of War' were written actually in the trenches. 'Kneeshaw Goes to War' was written before the end of the war[1] and published in 1919 in a volume entitled *Naked Warriors*. 'The End of a War' was composed as late as 1932 and first published in *The Criterion* for April 1933. The remaining two poems of this series, 'My Company' and 'The Execution of Cornelius Vane', belong to the war period, and are included in the 1919 volume.

In 'The Scene of War' Read still adhered closely to Imagist principles. These short poems are formally perfect, classically objective word-pictures of reality. The Imagists' indifference to subject-matter appears in his treatment of the horror and desolation of war. The cathartic effect of these poems is indicated by the lines of H. D. which Read prefixed to his 'Scene of War':

> 'And perhaps some outer horror,
> some hideousness to stamp beauty
> a mark
> on our hearts.'

Read's war poetry is exactly opposite to that of Wilfred Owen who thought that 'The Poetry is in the pity'.[2] When Read describes the havoc of war in 'Villages démolis', the pitiful fate of 'The Refugees', or the derision of 'The Crucifix', he does not want to stir our feelings of pity and indignation; he on the contrary endeavours to transmute these feelings into art. Here again he prays for the white flower of evolvèd calmness to enfold our hearts.

For the success of Read's artistic purpose it appears necessary that he should treat some large objective theme, some 'outer horror'; for when he chooses for his subject some inner experience of war he fails. Thus, 'Liedholz' is merely a *fait divers* which sounds unnecessarily emphatic when told in verse; in fact, the prose version of the same event in *Ambush* makes much better reading.[3] 'Fear' is little more than a 'conceit', and 'The Happy Warrior' a naturalistic study with a satirical implication.

[1] Originally published in *Art and Letters*, Vol. I (1918), pp. 125–131.
[2] See *The Poems of Wilfred Owen*, ed. by E. Blunden. Chatto and Windus, 1933, p. 40.
[3] Published as 'Criterion Miscellany, No. 16'. Faber & Faber, 1930, pp. 36 ff.

Read must have felt that the complexity and depth of the inner experience of war could only be handled in a longer poem. 'Knee-shaw Goes to War', 'My Company', and 'The Execution of Cornelius Vane' are progressive steps towards that end. But it is only in 'The End of a War' that Read achieves the desired impersonal beauty. Here, too, the poetry is not in the pity; but pity is not banished from the poetry as it is from 'The Scene of War'. What makes 'The End of a War' one of the few very great war poems is less its poetic form (there are some weak lines in it) than the wide range of thought and emotion which it gathers up in a perfectly adequate dramatic situation. The detachment with which the poet formerly transmuted the 'outer horror' into art is here brought to bear upon the highly complex inner experience of war. None of its essential aspects is sacrificed, neither the German officer's fanatic devotion to his vision of power and glory, nor the French girl's equally single-minded love of her country. There is no trace left of the superior, or didactic, or satirical attitudes which marred the earlier longer war poems. Out of the complex emotion of the whole poem one particular thought emerges which is worth examining as it shows a curious development in the poet's later life. In the final passage of the 'Meditation of the Waking English Officer' he writes:

> 'When first this fury caught us, then
> I vowed devotion to the rights of men
> would fight for peace once it came again
> from this unwilled war pass gallantly
> to wars of will and justice.'

This idealistic determination did not stand the test of actual war. For thus he continues:

> 'That was before I had faced death
> day in day out, before hope had sunk
> to a little pool of bitterness.
> Now I see, either the world is mechanic force
> and this the last tragic act, portending
> endless hate and blind reversion
> back to the tents and healthy lusts
> of animal men: or we act
> God's purpose in an obscure way.
> Evil can only to the Reason stand
> in scheme or scope beyond the human mind.'

From this apparent agnosticism Read has since returned to his former faith. Another war, the Spanish Civil War of 1936 to 1939, seemed to be a war 'of will and justice', and therefore justified. Read who hated the last war 'from the minute it began until the end'[1] thinks now again that 'The rational opponent of war . . . is not a pacifist, for he believes that there are ideals for which in the last resort he must wage war.'[2] This attitude might have resulted in war poems of an entirely different inspiration. Indeed, 'Bombing Casualties in Spain', 'Herschel Grynsban', and 'A Song for the Spanish Anarchists'[3] are filled with a warmer, more generous emotion than the poems inspired by the war of 1914 to 1918. With the collapse of the Government party in Spain, however, this new inspiration seems to have come to an end.

3. Satirical Verses (1919–1934)

Read was born in 1893, that is, eight years after Ezra Pound, seven years after H. D., five years after T. S. Eliot, and one year after Richard Aldington. He is, therefore, the youngest of the Imagist poets. This may explain why his own poetical development followed at a distance of several years that of Imagism proper. Thus the two principal phases to be distinguished in the Imagist movement were repeated by Read about five years later. The first Imagist phase lasted from about 1910 to 1914. The predominantly technical and aesthetic preoccupations of the Imagists of that stage are reflected in the work of T. E. Hulme, in Ezra Pound's 'A Few Don'ts',[4] and in the same poet's *Ripostes*.[5] Read's 'Eclogues' and 'The Scene of War', although they were written from 1914 to 1919, correspond to this first phase of Imagism.

The second phase lasted from 1914 to about 1920. It may be considered to have started with the two first and only numbers of *Blast* published on June 20, 1914, and July 1915, a short-lived periodical founded by Wyndham Lewis and Ezra Pound. This second phase may perhaps no more be called Imagism proper, but, if a name is wanted, should be remembered as Vorticism. It is characterised by a revulsion from the timeless beauty of nature or Greek mythology, or Chinese or Japanese scenery, to the very definite and actual aspects of Western civilisation, and by the shifting of attention from an almost exclusive care about form to a greater preoccupation with truth. Eliot's 'Preludes I-IV' and 'Rhapsody on a Windy Night'

---

[1] *Poetry and Anarchism*, Faber & Faber, 1938, p. 100.   [2] Ibid., p. 109.

[3] In *Thirty-Five Poems*, Faber & Faber, 1940.

[4] Published in *Poetry*, for March 1913.

[5] First published by Elkin Mathews, London, 1915.

were published in *Blast* for July 1915. Pound's *Lustra* appeared in 1916.[1] The outstanding feature of the new phase is its satirical bent. It is only now that the influence of Laforgue and Tailhade becomes really important. Satire, understood in its widest sense and directed rather against the Post-War world than against human frailties generally, was from now on a major current in English verse. The chief exponent during the nineteen-twenties was T. S. Eliot, but, in the words of Michael Roberts, between the years 1920 and 1928 'many poets were trying to write long poems which would present a unified view of the social crisis as they saw it, and imply their criticism of it'.[2]

For an understanding of Herbert Read's satirical verse it is necessary to realise the entirely unorthodox or 'anarchist' nature of his ideas of good and evil. His experience tells him 'that an ethical code is an imaginative and perhaps an irrational vision of conduct. It is an immediate or direct apprehension by the intelligence, and not the work of the discursive reason'.[3] As soon as the mind begins consciously to work out a system of ethical principles it is liable to error. This, I believe, is the idea to which Read has tried to give poetic expression in the first of his satirical poems, entitled 'Equation, $a+b+c=x$'.[4] The first three stanzas of this poem are three different statements of one intuition, namely of the essential identity and totality of (a) the world and God, (b) of man and woman, and (c) of the mind and its biological soil, the human body. The other half of the equation (x) is a query which might be formulated thus: How is it possible for the mind to manufacture a system of ethics outside the totality of the universe? Clearly, it is impossible. Any attempt to manufacture such a system by the mind alone without taking full account of the mind's opposite is condemned to inefficiency, like an engine 'accelerating in the void'.

Read would explain metaphysical poetry by the fact that 'thought is accelerated to the speed or intensity of emotion' which are

---

[1] See Réne Taupin, *op. cit.*, pp. 144 f.

[2] See Michael Roberts in his introduction to *The Faber Book of Modern Verse*, 1936, pp. 17 f. He enumerates Conrad Aiken's *Senlin* (1918), T. S. Eliot's *The Waste Land* (1922), Richard Aldington's *Fool i' the Forest* (1925), and Archibald MacLeish's *Hamlet of A. MacLeish* (1928). He might have added Osbert Sitwell, *England Reclaimed, a Book of Eclogues* (1927).

[3] *Reason and Romanticism*, 1926. From the essay on 'The Attributes of Criticism', p. 24.

[4] The explanation offered by Michael Roberts in *Critique of Poetry* (Cape, 1934, pp. 84 f.) is not convincing.

normally a thousand times greater than those of thought.[1] But the difficulty of such a poem as 'Equation' seems to be less in the speed, intensity, or complexity of the thought, than in the wilful oddness and surprising eccentricity of vocabulary, imagery, and style. The idea that ethical good is a matter of intuition and not of discursive reason is one of the 'great commonplaces' of all poetry.[2] That Read preferred his own modernist style when he was faced with the task of expressing this idea to a more traditional manner may be due to the same motive which caused Eliot to clothe his religious ideas in 'The Waste Land' in anthropological and Buddhist conceptions.[3]

Most of Read's satirical poems are directed against man's reluctance or inability to follow whole-heartedly his natural intuitions and healthy instincts. In 'The Brown Book of the Hitler Terror' he shows up, if I understand it rightly, the inconsistency of our romantic heroism and noble attitudes on the one hand, and our timidity and prudent discretion on the other. In the 'Short Poem for Armistice Day', which is probably the finest of his satires, the poet finds a poignant image and haunting rhythm to bring home his feeling of anticlimax at the sight of armistice celebrations, artificial poppies, crippled and disabled soldiers, of inane gestures and dead symbols, after all that has happened in the war. The line

'I have no power therefore have patience'

forms a melancholy echo to the waking English officer's evocation of the 'wandering wavering grace of humble men'. 'Lepidoptera', 'A Maiden's Comedy', and 'Ritz (Love among the Ruins)' are poetical 'five-finger exercises': 'Lepidoptera' reminds one of Corbière, the two other, with their abrupt and pungent ending, may have been influenced by Tailhade. 'Huskisson in Arcadia' is the first section of a longer poem entitled 'Huskisson Sacred and Profane. Another Jest too deep for Laughter', first published in *Coterie, A Quarterly*, for December 1919. This poem, as well as 'Tourists in a Sacred Place' and 'Picaresque', is satire of an inferior kind.

[1] *Reason and Romanticism*, p. 58. From the essay on 'The Nature of Metaphysical Poetry'. This essay was first published in 1923.

[2] See E. M. W. Tillyard, *Poetry Direct and Oblique*. Chatto and Windus, 1934, pp. 22–36.

[3] See Cleanth Brooks, *Modern Poetry and the Tradition*. The University of North Carolina Press, 1939, pp. 170 f.

4. Lyrical Poems (1919–1934)

To appreciate Read's lyrical poems one should know something of his poetical theory. His Imagist principles have already been discussed. In metaphysical poetry he admired 'a bold interfusion of thought and actuality'.[1] He disputed the opinion that didactic poetry such as Dante's, Donne's, Chapman's and Wordsworth's, was unpoetical:

'The *Commedia* is the complete expression of a very complete mind—a mind that saw as much beauty in the *Summa* of St. Thomas Aquinas as in the episode of Paolo and Francesca, and did not find these beauties inconsistent.'[2]

These two kinds of beauty had to be reconciled. Reason and Romanticism had to be explained as two aspects of one thing. He was very much under the influence of T. S. Eliot who tried to effect a similar reconciliation of opposites by his adherence to tradition.[3] Read's own solution was that the conditions of both Reason and Romanticism were satisfied by the intuitive apprehension of universal truth. At first he was inclined to see such an apprehension principally in the universals of medieval philosophy. Later, when he had studied psycho-analysis, McDougall, and Whitehead, which must have been about the years 1924 to 1926, he substituted for the universals the modern conception of organism.[4]

All these attempts to find a complete synthesis failed. They failed, not only because Reason and Romanticism are ultimately contradictory terms, but because the contradiction was in Read's personality itself. He realised this only after a profound change had occurred in his outlook on life as well as in his personal circumstances.[5] His new viewpoint became gradually clearer especially through his works on art, and his study of Surrealism. Final clarity was attained, however, only after Read had completed his survey by the inclusion of the political and social field. Thus, after relating

[1] *Reason and Romanticism*, p. 46. From the essay on 'The Nature of Metaphysical Poetry'.

[2] Ibid., p. 47.

[3] The close resemblance of Read's and Eliot's outlook at the time has not yet been sufficiently recognised. In this respect, Read's essay on 'The Attributes of Criticism' is particularly revealing. The beginning of its paragraph four (p. 21 f.) might have been written by Eliot himself.

[4] See the author's *Studien zur englischen Literarkritik 1910–30*, Bochum-Langendreer, 1938, pp. 185–7.

[5] See Read's own explanation quoted by the author, *ibid.*, pp. 187 f.

the theory of anarchism to the universalism and realism of medieval philosophy, he makes the following distinction:

'The rule of reason—to live according to natural law—this is also the release of the imagination. We have two possibilities: to discover truth, and to create beauty. We make a profound mistake if we confuse these two activities, attempting to discover beauty and to create truth. If we attempt to create truth, we can only do so by imposing on our fellow men an arbitrary and idealistic system which has no relation to reality; and if we attempt to discover beauty we look for it where it cannot be found—in reason, in logic, in experience. Truth is in reality, in the visible and tangible world of sensation; but beauty is in unreality, in the subtle and unconscious world of the imagination. If we confuse these two worlds of reality and imagination, then we breed not only national pride and religious fanaticism, but equally false philosophies and the dead arts of the academies. We must surrender our minds to universal truth, but our imagination is free to dream; is as free as the dream; is the dream.'[1]

Some of Read's lyrical poems show the influence of Eliot: so 'Penumbra', 'Inbetweentimes', 'Early Astir',[2] and 'Night Ride'.

Another group consists of more personal and more original poems: 'The White Isle of Leuce', 'September Fires', 'Day's Affirmation', 'Night's Negation', 'Other', and 'Melville'. 'Melville' is probably the latest of these. Aesthetically, it belongs to the same category as Lear's nonsense verse or nursery rhymes. In all these poems, and particularly in 'Aubade', the personal quality, the newness is in the images and in the thought; whereas the rhythm and the phrasing show less invention. In 'Formal Incantation' Read compensates the lack of rhythmic distinction by the use of mythological imagery with a fairly obvious psycho-analytical symbolism.

The next group of lyrics contains interesting examples of verse inspired by painting or by painter's impressions. 'The Judgment of Michael', 'Legend (for Viola and Pianoforte: Bax)', 'Flight', 'Tenement', 'Giovanni di Paolo', and 'Tectiform' belong to this group. In some of them emotion and form are not free from conventional associations, so in 'The Judgment of Michael' and 'Legend'. The most original, emotionally complex and formally interesting poem

---

[1] Herbert Read, *Poetry and Anarchism*, Faber & Faber, 1938, p. 97.

[2] 'Early Astir' was first published in *Coterie*, Autumn 1920, p. 54. In subject and matter it reminds one of Eliot's 'Preludes' which were first published in *Blast*, July 1915. I do not understand the word 'Yarrol' in the second stanza.

is 'Tectiform'; a perfect example of a poem inspired by a vision of 'the innocent eye'.

Finally, there is a group of poems in which Read appears in what Professor Bullough thinks is his principal rôle, as a poet of abstractions. 'Abstract poetry' is not always synonymous with 'obscure poetry'. Most of these poems are clear, though condensed. When reading them, one may, if one likes, distil the thought out of the verse, for, as Read himself explains,

'ideas, with which we have been obsessed during the activity of thought, may, when conscious thought is for the time being superseded by instinctive modes of expression, so guide such expression that it corresponds to the latent thought.'[1]

Thus we may deduce from 'Sic et Non' and 'Time Regained' that the poet—perhaps after meditating on his war experience or after reading Proust—had had certain intuitions of the relations of mind and body, of memory and experience, or of the part played by time in our spiritual life. But this is not essential. It is not the abstract thought that matters; what alone is important is the poem itself, the myth, the force and incantation of the words. Thus 'The Complaint of Heloise' is a vivid dramatic monologue which one remembers chiefly for a certain quality of voice. Its companion-piece, 'The Portrait of Abelard', is less successful: only the first and third stanza show anything of the same intensity.

The two poems 'Device' and 'Hulk' may have sprung from meditations on the contrast of two states of mind: the despondency of ordinary existence, and the glory of ecstatic vision. 'The Even Skein' reminds one of the beginning of Eliot's 'Burnt Norton' where similar motives of unrealised desires, of unachieved ideals are active. 'The Seven Sleepers' is weak; the myth lacks emotional power, the verse lacks distinction. It is not clear why Read included it among his *Thirty-Five Poems*. A much better poem is 'The Innocent Eye': it combines precise thinking with sympathy and with a very personal feeling of almost religiously fervent curiosity. The last two poems, 'Logos' and 'A Northern Legion', are really war poems. 'Logos' begins beautifully, but the first stanza ends with a limp line. 'A Northern Legion' is the 'vision divine and precise' of the fate of the soldier who is, as it were, trapped or ambushed by war.[2] This poem

[1] Herbert Read, *Surrealism*, Faber & Faber, 1936, p. 79.

[2] As far as may be ascertained, this poem was first published as an epigraph to a number of prose narratives of war experience which appeared in 1930 under the title of *Ambush* (*Criterion Miscellany*, No.16). 'To a Conscript of 1940' was first published in book form in *Thirty-Five Poems*, 1940.

should be read side by side with 'To a Conscript of 1940' written ten years later.

5. Longer Poems (1920–1934)

The theme of Read's first longer poem, 'The Analysis of Love', may be explained with reference to 'The Extasie' of John Donne, the more so as Read placed it under this motto: 'Else a great Prince in prison lies.'[1] Donne speculates about the hierarchy of which pure souls and human bodies are the extreme ends:

> 'As our blood labours to beget
>   Spirits, as like soules as it can,
> Because such fingers need to knit
>   That subtile knot, which makes us man:
> So must pure lovers soules descend
>   T'affections, and to faculties,
> Which sense may reach and apprehend,
>   Else a great Prince in prison lies.
> To our bodies turne wee then, that so
>   Weake men on love reveal'd may looke;
> Loves mysteries in soules doe grow,
>   But yet the body is his booke.'

Read contrasts lust and other bodily forms of love which may be apprehended rationally, with the mind's emotion, love:

> 'But your appeal is imperceptible
>   As ultimate atoms
> And the fast matrix
>   Of all within the human universe.'

The bodily forms of love, the emotions of love, a loving look, could be wrongly interpreted as 'the corrupted semblance of despair', as 'the anguish of love' but for the poet's knowledge that all these 'frailties germinant In a mind emotion-bound' are part of the mainspring of all life. They are merely 'drops we can absorb In the fount and flow of a passionless mood'. Having analysed love in its aspect of human littleness, in a mind emotion-bound, the poet then considers it in its purest form: mental ecstasy. Reason may be a vain

[1] Professor Bullough's comment that 'The Analysis of Love' 'is the analysis of the mind's isolation' (*The Trend of Modern Poetry*, Oliver and Boyd, 3rd ed., 1941, p. 122) does not seem to define the main theme of the poem.

endeavour to impose an order on the ever changing, crumbling world. As a materialist the poet knows that he will 'not avoid the avalanche', for

> 'Nature has perpetual tears
> In drooping boughs,
> And everywhere inanimate death
> Is immemorial.'

In mental ecstasy, however, the soul lovingly creates its own perfect universe where man may enjoy—at least while he has life—freedom, order, beauty, and the joys of creation.

The general movement of this poem is characteristic of most of the longer poems by Read; only 'The Lament of Saint Denis' makes an exception. It is a movement upward from the sense of limitation to an affirmation of freedom. Many of the great Romantic odes show the same development. It may be observed also in Read's next longer poem, 'Beata l'alma', which begins with the many causes of 'the mind's misanthropy' and leads up to a vision of a new type of man created to live in timeless reality. The first section of this poem would give a finer, more unified effect without the last two stanzas; the second section is less intense, but formally more satisfactory than the first.

The tone of 'The Retreat' is more subdued, more elegiac. The poet meditates on the mind, the heart, and the world, in a moment of quietness. The dominant mood is one of unreality and detachment. His former self, especially 'the fiendish days' of battle when the mind was 'passively receiving The body's ritual' is contrasted with the inner experience of more recent years, 'these agonies, wrung from the utterly fragile Frame of human life'. In view of man's littleness, these agonies are

> 'Perspectively doomed and wrought
> To the little loudness of an insect's cry.'

Nevertheless, the heart remains unsatisfied and melancholy, nor does the mind come to rest in universal harmony. The only rest is in the retreat into death where we shall again become one with

> '. . . the force
> Active even in the gulfs of uncreated space.'

Professor Bullough thinks that 'in this noble reflective poetry the reminiscences of Wordsworth serve to emphasise Mr. Read's divergence from romantic pantheism'.[1] The point is that in this poem Read

[1] *The Trend of Modern Poetry*, 1941, p. 123.

does not so much diverge from as coincide with romantic pantheism. We do not know when 'The Retreat' was composed; but it seems likely that it was written at a time when Read was studying the modern philosophy of organism.[1] All the points on which Wordsworth and Shelley agree in their attitude towards science and nature, are also part of Read's basic convictions. When he wrote this poem with its manifest analogies with Henry Vaughan and Wordsworth, Read had moved far away from his early Imagist style. What would T. E. Hulme have thought of it? Read does not fly away into the circumambient gas, but he does desire to drown himself in the 'something far more deeply interfused'. Perhaps Hulme would have been cynical enough not to see the difference.

The next poem, 'Mutations of the Phoenix', may be interpreted as an attempt at the reconciliation of romantic and classical tendencies. The romantic sense of integral unity with the all-pervading 'extensive energy'[2] is united with the desire for clear, disciplined concentration upon finite events, 'reflected interaction of any elements'. The poem begins with an act of liberation from morbid introspection, for

'. . . only the whorlminded Hamlet walks there
        musing in the gutters.'

Re-birth, metamorphosis, perfection are possible only in consciousness, not the consciousness of the egocentric individual but of the race, of Reason. As the phoenix rises from the flames, so the artist's vision is evolved from the burning uneasiness of the mind: not the uneasiness of an introspective, romantic, emotional Hamlet, but the nobler unrest of the searching intellect. Section five appears in parts redundant; but the whole of section seven is important. There we find Read's inmost thought, all his fundamental convictions, expressed exactly and powerfully: delight in clear finite things, delight in freedom from emotional deception, and an almost religious ardour in his prayer for clearness of vision.

'The Lament of Saint Denis', first published in *The New Criterion* for October 1926, is the finest of Read's longer poems. If I interpret it rightly (and I know that other interpretations are possible), it ex-

---

[1] In reviewing Whitehead's *Science and the Modern World* for *The New Criterion* of June 1926, Read called attention to the prominent place of aesthetics in this philosophy and to the categories of religion and art as defined by Whitehead. See the author's *Studien zur englischen Literarkritik 1910–30*, 1938, pp. 172–3, 185–9.

[2] See 'In Retreat', line 48.

presses in the form of a myth the poet's fear of all the forces that prevent re-birth, perfection, truth, and beauty, and which always lead back to 'chaos and dark nothingness'. The figure of Saint Denis is the symbol of enigmatic, contradictory reality in which those forces are at work. The children of light who seek

'With whirlpool eyes that are innocent'

embodiment in the ever changing and deceptively beautiful moments of actuality will also be engulfed in the inexorable chaos. The horror of this fatal event is evoked in one of the most haunting images of modern poetry:

'Our child is lost
in dream I have seen
a black bat laced
to his dead white face.'

The last of Read's *Poems 1914-1934* is entitled 'The Nuncio'. It was probably written about the time when he was preparing his book on *Art and Industry, the Principles of Industrial Design* (Faber & Faber 1934). It is a complex allegory, combining satire, humour, passionate reasoning, prophecy, and witty epigram. The thought is less intense than in the preceding longer poems, but the dramatic situation which forms the pattern of the work makes for greater ease of communication. Read's work as a professor of fine arts and as an interpreter of art to the public generally may have influenced the style of this poem towards greater conformity with ordinary (as opposed to poetic and imaginative) logic.

6. Conclusion

It appears from a study of Herbert Read's poetry as well as of his prose works that his personality combines the talent of the poet-philosopher with that of the poet-artist. He has the desire for knowledge and the capacity for abstract argument which characterise the man of science and the philosopher; but he also has the artist's quick and highly specialised sensitiveness to outward shapes. His feelings are aroused not only by the eternal themes of nature, love, death, and religion, but also by the logical implications of modern physics, of organic mechanism, and of certain psychological discoveries. On the other hand, pure sense impressions (not altered by literary or other extraneous associations) equally speak to his affections and give him intuitions of a profounder reality.

These two modes of thinking are not always reconciled in Read's poetry. Between 1919 and 1926 he wrote verse which wås mainly inspired by philosophical and scientific thought. Judging from the presumable date when some of his poems were written, it would seem that Eliot's influence was strongest in the early half of this period, whereas the poetry composed during the latter half shows signs of Read's interest in more modern trends of thought. During these seven years he probably also wrote most of his satirical verse. Read's failure to write a sustained and comprehensive satirical poem is probably due to the distrust with which he regarded the speculations and regulations of 'the ethic mind' and to his predominant interest in either the *Gestalt* of abstract thought or in the poetic value of sense impressions. Another reason may be seen in the comparative lateness with which he always followed the general movement of poetry. Thus, when he might have attained the maturity of judgment required for an enterprise of the magnitude of *The Waste Land*, the general conditions for such a poem had vanished.

The difference between Read's philosophical poetry and his other lyrical verse is defined by himself:

'Metaphysical poetry is determined logically: its emotion is a joy that comes with the triumph of reason, and is not a simple instinctive ecstasy. It is, finally, but the precise statement of such abstractions as the poet derives from his experience.'[1]

A lyric, therefore, is a poem that arouses 'a simple instinctive ecstasy' and 'in its purest state is concerned with the direct awareness of phenomenal environment'.[2] Read's poem 'The Innocent Eye' is the fullest and most precise illustration of this definition. The way in which Read's awareness of the outer world became gradually more delicate and complex may be studied in such poems as 'Pasturelands', 'Cranach', 'Flight', 'Tectiform', and 'The Nuncio', which represent successive stages in the development of the poet-artist. This development might perhaps also be illustrated by comparison with D. H. Lawrence. Read's early 'Eclogues' are in spirit much nearer the poems of *Birds, Beasts and Flowers* (1923) than his later verse in the same vein. The greater artistic freedom and range attained by Read after 1930, as compared with Lawrence's relatively monotonous interpretation of living nature, may be seen from the fact that Read's expressionist nature poetry includes, apart from such Lawrentian verse as may be found in 'Day's Affirmation' or

[1] *Reason and Romanticism*, pp. 55 f.
[2] Ibid., p. 34.

'Night Ride', also entirely fanciful poems like 'Melville' and 'Aubade'. As another extension of poetry towards greater artistic freedom we may consider poems probably inspired by actual paintings such as 'The Judgment of Michael' or 'Giovanni di Paolo'. A certain hardness of outline and economy of diction bear evidence of Imagist discipline. In this respect they present an ideal contrast to ' "The Tempest" of Giorgione' by W. J. Turner which is an example of the latest and highest development of the Georgian style in poetry.

Not all of Read's lyrics show the same predominantly pictorial character. There are many in which other emotions are at least as important as the joy that comes with the vision of the 'innocent eye'. Thus 'The White Isle of Leuce', 'September Fires', 'Day's Affirmation', 'Night's Negation', 'The Falcon and the Dove', 'A Northern Legion', 'Bombing Casualties in Spain', 'To a Conscript of 1940', and 'Summer Rain' are more purely lyrical in the accepted sense of the term. They, too, show the peculiar hardness and dryness of some of the typically Imagist poems, and they always have that shyness or emotional virginity which characterises Read's personal style. Those who like their lyrical verse expansive, richly orchestrated and very explicit will find little to their taste in his poetry and they had better not waste their time trying to enjoy it. It may be doubted, however, if they can enjoy Wordsworth, for the Lake poet too achieves his finest effects by transmuting passion into impersonal things.

J. F. HENDRY

THE PHILOSOPHY OF HERBERT READ

The philosophy of Herbert Read may conveniently be considered for the purposes of this essay, under three headings: political, general, and 'organic', but it is essential to note that of these the key word is 'organic', and that both in his general outlook, and in his search for a satisfactory social system, Herbert Read remains true to his individual vision and organic experience.

It is possible to argue, as has been done already in the case of Rainer Maria Rilke, that Herbert Read is concerned solely or mainly with aesthetic experience. This approach has its uses, in that it enables those of us who dislike effort, to dismiss him along with Rilke, as an 'aesthete', or even as a mystic. In fact the aesthetic experience with Read is but a part of experience. Nor have we, strictly speaking, the right, from the point of view of his philosophy, to label it 'aesthetic' at all, since by so doing we smudge the purity of the image. Experience, the whole of experience, is thus a vital factor in any consideration of Read's philosophy and we shall do well not to prejudge matters.

No one of his books is concerned with philosophy alone, and formulation of it is therefore difficult. Always, however, the philosophy is latent, or expressed, and in occasional volumes may even be the dominating theme. Thus in *Poetry and Anarchism*, *Form in Modern Poetry*, *Annals of Innocence and Experience*, and *The Green Child*, there are many useful and direct clues as to the philosophical development of the writer.

His first introduction to anything approaching a philosophical system came with the discovery of Nietzsche, and however this German's ideas may have been discarded later, the influence probably remains in so far as Read's philosophy is *dynamic*, in a constant state of growth like man himself. In quick succession he passed on to the indiscriminate reading of Schopenhauer, Kant, Hegel, Hume, Pascal and Plato, absorbing doubtless something from each which he made his own. We may fancy we see in his encouragement of surrealism the influence of Hume's epiphenomenalism; in his highly individual religious sense, the feelings of Pascal; in his uncompromising if gentle anarchism, the striving toward the ideal republic of Plato; but this is to do less than justice to Read himself. Too often does literary criticism regard the lives of writers as the history of ideas, but artists are not inanimate puppets juggling with extraneous thoughts, as with balls. In each of them, thought, life and experience are continually acting upon each other and upon the past. If Read has seen fit to encourage surrealism it need not be because he 'believed' in it; still less because he remembered his Hume; but merely because it seemed to give expression to a section of human life hitherto ignored, the subconscious. No one believing as does Read in the essential significance of the individual life in every aspect, could do other.

He does not believe in a superman, like Nietzsche, but he sees no reason at present to consider man's potentialities limited and finite. He gives his loyalty neither to the materialism of Marx nor to the idealism of Hegel, though wisely attributing much of the truth to both of these men, because he feels himself alive and therefore somehow outside of their systems by that very fact. In this he is in the tradition of English empiricism, one of the greatest revolutionary forces in our modern civilisation.

Similarly, and doubtless for the same reason, he acknowledges the influence of such thinkers as Bergson, Whitehead, Croce, and especially Vico, whilst renouncing any share in their general outlook. On the other hand he finds himself in 'emotional' rather than intellectual sympathy with writers like Traherne, Kierkegaard and Santayana, though again not necessarily sharing their conclusions. Here I cannot do better than quote:

'Though I still read metaphysics when it comes my way or suits my mood, I have been prevented from becoming a metaphysician by a strong feeling that anything not evident to our senses, or to the extension of our senses provided by scientific instruments, is not of great importance to our lives. Even scientific speculations cease to interest me when they can only be handled by means of mathematical symbols. If I cling to a realm of supermaterial values, which Santayana calls the Realm of Essence, it is because the existence of such values is as evident to my senses as sticks and stones.'

This passage is interesting, though one may not share the ideas expressed entirely, because it does delimit with some exactitude the area covered by Read's philosophy. Implied is the very important conception that life is to be lived if we are to find an answer to its problems; that we are unlikely to discover anything outside of ourselves and the familiar world which will provide us with a magic

key, whether in the form of a scientific formula or a political shibbo-
leth. In this intensity of living he discovers the truth of Traherne's
dictum:

'It is of the nobility of man's soul that he is insatiable,' and adds,
'The senses are God's instruments, and we minister to his power and
goodness with these divine engines. We thus acquire a sense of the
glory which is immanent in the world and which we live to exploit,
like veins of gold in the dull ore of experience.'

An echo of this transcendentalism Read finds again in the
Journals of Kierkegaard: 'something which grows together with the
deepest roots of my life, through which I am, so to speak, grafted
upon the divine'.

Common to all of these influences, it will be seen, is the feeling
of the goodness of nature and the value of organic life, emotion,
experience and intellect, as a whole, together with the freedom to
develop these to the full.

As might have been expected therefore, Herbert Read has
declared politically for anarchism, not, it is true, in any immediate
sense, for human perfection is not to be achieved overnight, but
rather as the goal towards which society must strive. His sympathies
are with Bakunin, via Sorel and syndicalism, rather than with
Marx, where philosophy is concerned. Again the guiding conception is nothing more than his sense of loyalty toward the whole of
experience.

With socialist policy he may and usually does find himself in
agreement. There could be no more question of his opposing socialism in England than there was of the Spanish Anarchists fighting
against the Republic. For Read, however, it would be but a step towards that completer freedom which shall identify duty with joy,
and be devoid of compulsion. 'The true social faith', he has said, 'is
to work for the immediate practical objects of socialism, but at the
same time to keep before us, some ultimate ideal—some goal to
which we may aim', for 'anarchism does not believe in plans'. It
regards these as rational constructions which must perforce leave
out the elusive and imponderable factors of human feeling and
instinct.

'There is only one plan—the plan of nature. We must live according to natural laws, and by virtue of the power which comes from
concentrating upon their manifestation in the human mind. Anarchism asserts—it is its only assertion—that life must be so ordered that
the individual can live a natural life, "attending to what is within" . . .'

Here once more is revealed the man's implicit faith in the intrinsic value of the individual and organic life of experience, *for which there can be no substitute.*

For its sake, he is on the side of the liberating forces within societies and nations.

II

This intense awareness of each aspect of man's mysterious journey through space and time has led Herbert Read to enunciate in literary criticism an idea which is of some psychological and philosophical import as well, his favourite distinction between character and personality.

Something of the sort has been expressed before. Says Goethe: 'Es bildet ein Talent sich in der Stille; sich ein Charakter in dem Strom der Welt.' (Talent takes shape in quiet, character in the stream of the world.)

Read, however, has seen that talent has little to do with the point, that certain people are more readily adaptable to changing conditions than others. These he terms 'personalities'. 'Character is the product of a disciplined education: discipline inculcates habits of mind as well as of body, and the result is a firm, dependable set of ideas and reactions upon which a definite type of society can be based. A character is not necessarily conservative: rather it is constructive, and in a time of stress or disintegration might well seem revolutionary. It is moral, though its morality is not necessarily conventional. It cultivates a "taste", but this taste is rational rather than aesthetic, retrospective and historical rather than experimental and contemporary.

'A personality, on the other hand, is distinguished by immediacy and by what I would call lability, or the capacity to change without loss of integrity. Keats, who discerned the quality in himself, gave it the name of Negative Capability; and in Hamlet Shakespeare depicted the type in all its mutability.

'Character is only attained by limitation. The senses, which, would otherwise be open to the impact of every phenomenal event, must be canalised, protected by a hard cortex or shell, and only allowed to operate when they have been directed by the conscious will; and it can be argued that sensations and their attendant emotions are all the finer for being thus restricted. But the personality will have none of this arbitrary interference with the natural process of selectivity: the senses are open to every impression which falls upon

111

them, and the mind surrenders to its environment. Admittedly, from a moral and social point of view, there is a danger that such a passive attitude will lead to instability and disintegration. But the values of the personality are neither moral nor social: they are religious or aesthetic. Here the word "religious", put in contrast to "moral", may cause some surprise; but I would be prepared to maintain that the essentially religious experience described by the great mystics of the East as well as the West, and now generally known in modern theology as the Kierkegaardian "instinct", the Barthian "crisis" or "leap", is a surrender of the existential being only possible to a personality, a man of negative capability.

'To question the values of the personality, therefore, is to question the values of mysticism and of art. The greatest mistake would be to suppose that a society can be based exclusively on one type of human being. Society needs for vitality, and for effective progress, the contrast and opposition of types, more particularly of these two fundamental types which I have called characters and personalities. The tautness of the social fabric depends on their dialectical counterplay.'[1]

This is an extremely illuminating passage, since it illustrates both Read's knowledge of psychology and his appreciation of dialectical forces at work within, as well as outside of, the individual. This is more vital to his 'Weltanschauung' than may be at first realised. It is the basis of any belief in human betterment. Too often the classicist, the man of character, is to be found on the side of reaction, possibly because existing order guarantees his own inhibitions, answers the needs of his being. The romantic, on the other hand, the personality, is the embodiment of permanent revolution, and that in no narrow political sense. He is ever on the side of life, and that makes him individualist.

These two elements often reside in the same person. Thus we get the early and late Goethe; Tolstoy of *Resurrection* and of *War and Peace*; Yeats of the 'Celtic Twilight' and of 'Easter, 1916'. Equally both are necessary in the growth of society.

It is this rounded view of Read's which is really valuable, and may find a place in some future applied sociology.

He has termed himself 'romantic', but actually, in his poetry as in his philosophy, we are constantly aware of this dialectical interplay between reason and emotion, between rational, ordered judgment and the 'sense of glory'.

[1] *Annals of Innocence and Experience*, pp. 90-1.

It should be obvious from this that Read is an ardent believer in the spiritual, invisible world. Nevertheless even here he is checked by prudent reason—'the falcon' that broods on his wrist.

Reason dictates that he should not believe in personal survival after death. This, of course, is an extremely difficult subject, and 'survival' can mean widely-different things. Thus the Tibetan rejects the idea of any 'permanent ego'. At the same time he believes in the survival of consciousness, even 'consciousness of the I', on another plane.

Herbert Read appears to reason along much the same lines to judge by the following:

'Deep down in my consciousness is the consciousness of a collective life, a life of which I am a part and to which I contribute a minute but unique extension. When I die and fall, the tree remains, nourished to some small degree by my brief manifestation of life. Millions of leaves have preceded me and millions will follow me; the tree itself grows and endures. Some people can find no consolation in this symbol. They are the people who fear death—who can die comfortably only in the illusion that they will continue to live in another world, or on another plane of consciousness. If they can really maintain such an illusion they are welcome to it. . . . My own philosophy may be a similar illusion. . . .'

There is much that one could say with reference to this passage. The symbol of the tree is reminiscent of Rilke:

'O Bäume Lebens, o wann winterlich?'

but Rilke went much further in his exploration of the invisible world than Read. The tree, as such, was insufficient symbol for him. He did believe in existence on another plane, as the Tenth of his Duinese Elegies shows. Nor was this plane the purely ideal one which Read borrows from Santayana.

Nor is it fair to say that those who find no consolation in the symbol of the tree are those who fear death. It is after all only a metaphor, and in such abstruse matters anything like consistency on the part of the writer is not to be expected. I myself much prefer the following passage which actually seems to contradict the above.

'. . . everything shimmers for a second on the expanding rim of my memory. The farthest tremor of this perturbation is lost only at the finest edge where sensation passes beyond the confines of experience; for memory is a flower which only opens fully in the kingdom of heaven where the eye is eternally innocent.'

Either the world of abstract ideas, mathematical formulae, poems, and ideals has no reality whatever—in which case there is no invisible world at all and we are all deluding ourselves—or it has a real existence somewhere, one as real as our own, perhaps more so, in which case agnosticism, and disbelief in 'personal' immortality become things of very small moment if not actually meaningless. In this sphere Read's fundamental beliefs are difficult to grasp because he seems shy of utterance, but it does seem that he shares belief in survival of consciousness with Tibetan mystics, whilst denying that our essential selves are to be identified with our idiosyncrasies much as they deny the permanence of the 'ego'.

From his own organic point of view he ignores such phenomena as extra-sensory perception or telesthaesia, and there are aspects of inspiration and even of the poetic image which he overlooks. Nevertheless, no one in England recently, has followed a more consistent path, formed a more coherent philosophy, or done more, by intelligent anticipation and encouragement, to develop English poetry along its own native lines, and with it, English art and science.

His significance lies not in the fact that he is a metaphysician. He himself has denied that. Nor has he built up any philosophical system, perhaps because of an innate distrust of systems. He is unique in that his philosophy is his life, and his life his philosophy. The one grows and flourishes with the other. Few men give the impression of having lived so fully, and yet so carefully, so deeply and yet with such awareness.

It is impossible therefore to state Read's philosophy in any series of dicta. Its basic tenets are living, and they are these: the child-like eye sees truth because it is innocent; it is the task of the artist or philosopher to recover that innocence because of the vision of sharp truth it brings him; that primal innocence and truth is like a ray illuminating and giving meaning to all subsequent experience. Hence it follows that every man has his own truth within him, his own phantasy or myth to be fulfilled, and that the vision of innocence will help him to fulfil it, to grow into completeness, to grow—or 'die' if we like—into that invisible world which is the kingdom of heaven, but with perfect naturalness, with perfect grace. If there is consciousness there, and memory does flower again, that shall indeed be the highest of immortalities.

This is the extent of Read's greatness then, that he has shown us something of how life should be lived, according to the law of nature, even of our own inmost nature, and that he has grafted that nature of ours on to the supernatural, the divine. He has shown us—not a system—but a process of constant flowering, of which he himself is an example.

He has also, which is equally important, freed his fellows to develop as he has done. He has shown 'The Way', and made it clear that their own 'Ways' need not at all be the same, but that they will nevertheless form part of the great Scheme. The philosophy, the politics, which were of personal import, become of national import, precisely because they have been so sincerely held and lived. Thus, it may be hoped, the kingdom of God, which is within, may some day be manifest in the outer world, for such is the significance and inspiration of Read's message.

SELECT BIBLIOGRAPHY

(This list includes all works published in separate book form: it does not include works to which the author was a contributor, nor various volumes to which he has contributed introductions. American editions are only included if substantially different from the English editions.)

1. SONGS / OF CHAOS / BY / HERBERT READ / 'One must have chaos within one to give birth to / a dancing star'—NIETZSCHE / LONDON / ELKIN MATHEWS, CORK STREET / MCMXV. Pp. 38, $7\frac{1}{4} \times 5$.

2. ECLOGUES / A BOOK OF POEMS / HERBERT READ. (No imprint on title-page; colophon: 'Here ends Eclogues a Book of Poems / by Herbert Read The Cover and the Decorations / designed by Ethelbert White The Typography / and Binding arranged by Cyril W. Beaumont / Printed by hand on his Press at 75 Charing / Cross Road in the City of Westminster / Completed December the Twentieth / MDCCCCXIX.' Pp. 38, $7\frac{1}{2} \times 5$.

3. NAKED / WARRIORS / BY / HERBERT READ / And there were some that / went into the battle naked / and unarmed, fighting / only with the fervour of / their spirit, dying and / getting many wounds / 1919 / ART & LETTERS / 9 DUKE STREET / ADELPHI, LONDON, W.C.2. Printed at the Pelican Press. Pp. 60, $7 \times 4\frac{1}{2}$.

4. AUGURIES / OF LIFE & DEATH / Written in Memory of / CHARLES READ / Lieutenant of The Yorkshire Regiment / Born April 24th 1897 / Killed in action at Beaurevoir in France / October 5th 1918. Privately printed, n.d. (1919). Pp. 8, $7 \times 4\frac{1}{2}$.

5. MUTATIONS OF / THE PHOENIX / HERBERT READ / PRINTED AND PUBLISHED BY LEONARD & VIRGINIA WOOLF / AT THE HOGARTH PRESS / HOGARTH HOUSE RICHMOND / 1923. Pp. 52, $9\frac{3}{4} \times 7\frac{1}{4}$.

6. ENGLISH POTTERY / ITS DEVELOPMENT FROM EARLY TIMES / TO THE END OF THE EIGHTEENTH CENTURY / BY / BERNARD RACKHAM / AND / HERBERT READ / BOTH OF THE VICTORIA AND ALBERT MUSEUM / WITH AN APPENDIX ON THE WROTHAM POTTERS / BY / DR. J. W. L. GLAISHER, F.R.S. / The art plastic was moulding in clay, or potters' / earth

anciently. This is the parent of statuary, sculpture, / graving, and picture; cutting in brass and marble, all / serve under her. BEN JONSON, *Discoveries*, CXXI. / MCMXXIV / LONDON: ERNEST BENN, LIMITED / 8 BOUVERIE STREET, E.C.4. Pp. 144 + cxv plates, $11\frac{1}{4} \times 8\frac{1}{2}$.

7. SPECULATIONS / ESSAYS ON HUMANISM AND / THE PHILOSOPHY OF ART / By / T. E. HULME / Edited by / HERBERT READ / With a Frontispiece and Foreword by / JACOB EPSTEIN / LONDON / KEGAN PAUL, TRENCH, TRUBNER & CO., LTD. / NEW YORK: HARCOURT, BRACE & COMPANY, INC. / 1924. Pp. 272, $8\frac{1}{2} + 5\frac{1}{4}$.

8. IN RETREAT / BY / HERBERT READ / Published by / Leonard & Virginia Woolf at The Hogarth Press / 52 Tavistock Square, London, W.C.1 / 1925. Pp. 44, $8\frac{1}{2} \times 5\frac{1}{4}$.

9. REASON AND / ROMANTICISM / Essays in Literary Criticism / *By* HERBERT READ / *Homo est quodammodo omnia* / —ST / THOMAS AQUINAS / Faber and Gwyer. (1926). Pp. 250, $7\frac{1}{4} \times 5$.

10. ENGLISH / STAINED GLASS / BY / HERBERT READ / OF THE VICTORIA AND ALBERT MUSEUM / LONDON & NEW YORK / G. P. PUTNAM'S SONS. (October 1926). Pp. 260, ill., $11\frac{1}{4} \times 8\frac{1}{2}$.

11. COLLECTED POEMS / 1913-25 / *By* / Herbert / Read / LONDON / Faber and Gwyer / MCMXXVI. Pp. 116, $7\frac{3}{4} \times 5$.

12. ENGLISH PROSE / STYLE / BY / HERBERT READ / LONDON / G. BELL AND SONS, LTD. 1928. Pp. 228, $8\frac{3}{4} \times 5\frac{3}{4}$.

13. PHASES OF / ENGLISH POETRY / BY / HERBERT READ / Published by Leonard & Virginia Woolf at The / Hogarth Press, 52 Tavistock Square, London, W.C.1 / 1928. Pp. 158, $7\frac{1}{4} \times 4\frac{3}{4}$.

14. *The Sense of Glory* / ESSAYS / IN CRITICISM / BY / HERBERT READ / Wer das Tiefste gedacht, liebt das Lebendigste / HÖLDERLIN / CAMBRIDGE / AT THE UNIVERSITY PRESS / 1929. Pp. 228, $8\frac{3}{4} \times 5\frac{1}{2}$.

15. A SENTIMENTAL / JOURNEY / *By* LAURENCE STERNE / Edited with an Introduction by / HERBERT READ. THE SCHOLARTIS PRESS / 30 MUSEUM STREET, LONDON, W.C.1 / 1929. Pp. xliv + 230, $7\frac{3}{4} \times 4\frac{1}{2}$.

16. Notes on Language / and Style / By / T. E. HULME / *Edited by Herbert Read* / 1929 / UNIVERSITY OF WASHINGTON BOOK STORE / Seattle. Pp. 28, $7\frac{1}{4} \times 4\frac{3}{4}$.

17. STAFFORDSHIRE / POTTERY FIGURES / BY / HERBERT READ / *Of*

the Victoria and Albert Museum / DUCKWORTH / 3 HEN-
RIETTA STREET, LONDON / 1929. Pp. 24 + 70 Pls., 11 × 8¼.

18. WORDSWORTH / The Clark Lectures / 1929-1930 / BY / HER-
BERT READ / LONDON / JONATHAN CAPE / TORONTO (1930).
Pp. 272, 7¾ × 5¼.

19. AMBUSH / BY / HERBERT READ / LONDON / FABER & FABER LTD.
/ 24 RUSSELL SQUARE (1930). Pp. 44, 7¾ × 5¼.

20. Julien Benda and the / NEW Humanism / By / HERBERT READ /
1930 / UNIVERSITY OF WASHINGTON BOOK STORE / Seattle.
Pp. 34, 7¼ × 4¾.

21. THE / MEANING OF ART / BY / HERBERT READ / *A true taste is
never a half taste.* / —Constable / LONDON / FABER &
FABER LIMITED / 24 RUSSELL SQUARE (1931). Pp. 159,
+46 figs. 7¼ × 4¾. (New and revised edition. 1935. Pp.
224 + 50 figs.)

22. THE PLACE OF ART IN / A UNIVERSITY / AN INAUGURAL LEC-
TURE GIVEN AT THE / UNIVERSITY OF EDINBURGH ON /
15TH OCTOBER, 1931 / BY HERBERT READ / WATSON
GORDON PROFESSOR OF FINE ART / OLIVER AND BOYD /
EDINBURGH: TWEEDALE COURT / LONDON: 33 PATERNOSTER
ROW, E.C. / 1931. Pp. 28, 7½ × 5.

23. THE LONDON BOOK / OF / ENGLISH PROSE / SELECTED AND
ORDERED BY / HERBERT READ AND BONAMY DOBREE /
LONDON / Eyre and Spottiswoode Ltd. / 1931. Pp.
xxxviii + 666, 7¼ × 4¾.

24. THE / ANATOMY OF ART / AN INTRODUCTION TO / THE PRO-
BLEMS OF ART / AND AESTHETICS / BY / HERBERT READ /
WATSON GORDON PROFESSOR OF FINE ARTS IN THE /
UNIVERSITY OF EDINBURGH / *Illustrated* / DODD, MEAD &
COMPANY / NEW YORK 1932. Pp. xii + 224 + 46 pls.,
8 × 5½. (The same work as No. 22 with additional material.

25. FORM IN / MODERN POETRY / BY / HERBERT READ / *Wer viel
lernen kann, ist kein Genie.* / EMIL NOLDE / LONDON /
SHEED & WARD / 1932. Pp. xiv + 82, 7¼ × 4½.

26. ART NOW / AN INTRODUCTION TO / THE THEORY OF MODERN /
PAINTING AND SCULPTURE / BY HERBERT READ / FABER
AND FABER LIMITED / LONDON 24 RUSSELL SQUARE W.C.1.
(1933). Pp. 144 + 128 pls., 8 × 5½.
(New and revised edition, 1936. Pp. 160 + 128 pls.)

27. THE INNOCENT EYE / BY HERBERT READ / LONDON / FABER &
FABER LTD. / 24 RUSSELL SQUARE. (April 1933). Pp. 82,
8 × 5¼.

28. THE / ENGLISH VISION / AN ANTHOLOGY / EDITED BY / READ / LONDON / Eyre & Spottiswoode Ltd. / 1933. Pp. xx + 364, $7\frac{1}{4} \times 5$.

29. THE END / OF A WAR / BY / HERBERT / READ / FABER AND / FABER. (November 1933.) Pp. 32, $8\frac{3}{4} \times 5\frac{1}{2}$.

30. ART AND INDUSTRY / the PRINCIPLES of INDUSTRIAL DESIGN by HERBERT READ / FABER & FABER, LIMITED / LONDON: 24 RUSSELL SQUARE / 1934. Pp. iv + 144 ill., $10 \times 7\frac{1}{2}$.

31. POEMS / 1914-1934 / HERBERT READ / LONDON / FABER & FABER. (February 1935.) Pp. 168, $8\frac{1}{2} \times 5\frac{1}{2}$.

32. IN DEFENCE OF SHELLEY / & / OTHER ESSAYS / BY / HERBERT READ / WILLIAM HEINEMANN LTD. / LONDON TORONTO / (1936.) Pp. viii + 282, $8\frac{1}{2} \times 5\frac{1}{2}$.

33. THE GREEN CHILD / A ROMANCE / BY / HERBERT READ / WILLIAM HEINEMANN LTD / LONDON TORONTO. (1935.) Pp. 256, $7\frac{1}{2} \times 5$.

34. SURREALISM / edited with an / introduction by / HERBERT / READ / contributions by / ANDRE BRETON / HUGH SYKES DAVIES / PAUL ELUARD / GEORGES HUGNET / FABER AND FABER LIMITED / 24 Russell Square London. (November 1936.) Pp. 252 + 96 illus., $8 \times 5\frac{1}{4}$.

35. ART AND SOCIETY / by Herbert Read / WILLIAM HEINEMANN LTD / London and Toronto. (1937.) Pp. xx + 282 ill., $8\frac{1}{4} \times 6\frac{1}{2}$.

36. COLLECTED ESSAYS / in Literary Criticism / by / HERBERT READ / FABER AND FABER LTD / 24 Russell Square / London. (October 1938.) Pp. 366, $8\frac{3}{4} \times 5\frac{1}{2}$.

37. POETRY / AND ANARCHISM / by / HERBERT READ / FABER AND FABER / 24 Russell Square / London. (June 1938.) Pp. 126, $8\frac{3}{4} \times 5\frac{1}{2}$.

38. The Knapsack / A pocket-book of Prose and Verse / EDITED BY / HERBERT READ / LONDON / GEORGE ROUTLEDGE & SONS, LTD. / BROADWAY HOUSE: CARTER LANE, E.C. (1939.) Pp. x + 622, $6\frac{1}{4} \times 4$.

39. ANNALS OF / INNOCENCE / AND / EXPERIENCE / BY / HERBERT / READ / FABER & FABER / LONDON. / (November 1940.) Pp. 212, $8\frac{1}{2} \times 5\frac{1}{2}$.

40. THIRTY-FIVE POEMS / by / HERBERT READ / Faber and Faber / 24 Russell Square / London. (November 1940.) Pp. 80, $7\frac{1}{4} \times 5$.

41. THE / PHILOSOPHY / OF / ANARCHISM / by / Herbert Read / FREEDOM PRESS DISTRIBUTORS / 9 Newbury Street / London, E.C.1 / 1940. Pp. 36, $8\frac{3}{4} \times 5\frac{1}{2}$.

42. To Hell with / Culture / Democratic Values are New Values / Herbert Read / London / Kegan Paul, Trench, Trubner & Co., Ltd. / Broadway House, 68-74 Carter Lane, E.C. (1941.) Pp. 64, 7½ × 4¾.
43. Kropotkin / *Selections from his Writings* / Edited with an Introduction by / Herbert Read / Freedom Press / London. (December 1942.) Pp. 150, 8¼ × 5½.
44. The Politics / of the Unpolitical / *Herbert Read* / Routledge / 1943. Pp. 160, 7¼ × 4¾.
45. Education / Through Art / by / Herbert Read / *I am simply calling attention to the / fact that fine art is the only teacher / except torture. Bernard Shaw* / Faber and Faber / 24 Russell Square / London. Pp. xxiv + 312 + 56 pls. (1943.) 8½ × 5½.

In the Press

Henry Moore. Sculptures and Drawings, edited with an Introduction by Herbert Read. London: Percy Lund, Humphries & Co.

An enlargement of: Henry Moore / Sculptor / An Appreciation by / Herbert Read / With Thirty-six Plates / 1934 / A. Zwemmer / Charing Cross Road, London W.C.2. Pp. 16 + 36 pls. 9½ × 7.

Paul Nash. Thirty-two reproductions of his work with an Introduction by Herbert Read. Penguin Books.